What You Need to Know about Eating Disorders

Recent Titles in
Inside Diseases and Disorders

What You Need to Know about Eating Disorders

Jessica Bartley and Melissa Streno

Inside Diseases and Disorders

BLOOMSBURY ACADEMIC
NEW YORK • LONDON • OXFORD • NEW DELHI • SYDNEY

BLOOMSBURY ACADEMIC

Bloomsbury Publishing Inc, 1359 Broadway, 12th Floor, New York, NY 10018, USA
Bloomsbury Publishing Plc, 50 Bedford Square, London, WC1B 3DP, UK
Bloomsbury Publishing Ireland, 29 Earlsfort Terrace, Dublin 2, D02 AY28, Ireland

BLOOMSBURY, BLOOMSBURY ACADEMIC and the Diana logo are
trademarks of Bloomsbury Publishing Plc

First published in the United States of America by ABC-CLIO 2020
Paperback edition published by Bloomsbury Academic 2025

Library of Congress Cataloging-in-Publication Data
Names: Bartley, Jessica, author. | Streno, Melissa, author.
Title: What you need to know about eating disorders / Jessica Bartley and Melissa Streno.
Description: Santa Barbara, California : ABC-CLIO, LLC, [2020] |
Series: Inside diseases and disorders | Includes bibliographical references and index.
Identifiers: LCCN 2019037885 (print) | LCCN 2019037886 (ebook) |
ISBN 9781440862397 (hardcover) | ISBN 9781440862403 (ebook)
Subjects: LCSH: Eating disorders—Treatment. | Eating disorders—
Patients—Family relationships. | Eating disorders—Case studies.
Classification: LCC RC552.E18 B373 2020 (print) | LCC RC552.E18 (ebook) |
DDC 616.85/26—dc23
LC record available at https://lccn.loc.gov/2019037885
LC ebook record available at https://lccn.loc.gov/2019037886

ISBN: HB: 978-1-4408-6239-7
PB: 979-8-2163-9264-4
ePDF: 978-1-4408-6240-3
eBook: 979-8-2161-6435-7

Series: Inside Diseases and Disorders

For product safety related questions contact productsafety@bloomsbury.com.

To find out more about our authors and books visit www.bloomsbury.com
and sign up for our newsletters.

We would like to dedicate this book to our growing daughters and the generation to come.

Contents

CHAPTER 8
Prevention *85*

CHAPTER 9
Issues and Controversies *95*

CHAPTER 10
Current Research and Future Directions *105*

Case Illustrations 117

Glossary 129

Directory of Resources 137

Index 143

Series Foreword

Disease is as old as humanity itself, and it has been the leading cause of death and disability throughout history. From the Black Death in the Middle Ages to smallpox outbreaks among Native Americans to the modern-day epidemics of diabetes and heart disease, humans have lived with—and died from—all manner of ailments, whether caused by infectious agents, environmental and lifestyle factors, or genetic abnormalities. The field of medicine has been driven forward by our desire to combat and prevent disease and to improve the lives of those living with debilitating disorders. And while we have made great strides forward, particularly in the last 100 years, it is doubtful that mankind will ever be completely free of the burden of disease.

Greenwood's Inside Diseases and Disorders series examines some of the key diseases and disorders, both physical and psychological, affecting the world today. Some (such as diabetes, cardiovascular disease, and ADHD) have been selected because of their prominence within modern America. Others (such as Ebola, celiac disease, and autism) have been chosen because they are often discussed in the media and, in some cases, are controversial or the subject of scientific or cultural debate.

Because this series covers so many different diseases and disorders, we have striven to create uniformity across all books. To maximize clarity and consistency, each book in the series follows the same format. Each begins with a collection of 10 frequently asked questions about the disease or disorder, followed by clear, concise answers. Chapter 1 provides a general introduction to the disease or disorder, including statistical information such as prevalence rates and demographic trends. The history of the disease or disorder, including how our understanding of it has evolved over time, is addressed in chapter 2. Chapter 3 examines causes and risk factors, whether genetic, microbial, or environmental, while chapter 4 discusses signs and symptoms. Chapter 5 covers the issues of diagnosis (and misdiagnosis), treatment, and management (whether with drugs, medical procedures, or lifestyle changes). How such treatment, or the lack thereof, affects a patient's long-term prognosis, as well as the risk of complications, are the subject of chapter 6. Chapter 7 explores the disease or disorder's effects on the friends and family of a patient—a dimension often overlooked in discussions of physical and psychological ailments. Chapter 8 discusses prevention strategies, while chapter 9 explores key issues or controversies, whether medical or sociocultural. Finally, chapter 10 profiles cutting-edge research and speculates on how things might change in the next few decades.

Each volume also features five fictional case studies to illustrate different aspects of the book's subject matter, highlighting key concepts and themes that have been explored throughout the text. The reader will also find a glossary of terms and a collection of print and electronic resources for additional information and further study.

As a final caveat, please be aware that the information presented in these books is no substitute for consultation with a licensed health care professional. These books do not claim to provide medical advice or guidance.

Acknowledgments

We would like to thank the faculty and staff of the Graduate School of Professional Psychology at the University of Denver for providing a phenomenal foundation in clinical work. Additionally, we would like to express gratitude for our incredible colleagues and mentors at EDCare. From supervision to peer consultation, we feel that we learned very much and would not have had the knowledge base and the skill set necessary to work with eating disorders without you! And finally, a big thank-you to our friends and family. This book would not have been possible without you either!

Introduction

Not only are eating disorders on the rise but, luckily, there is also a growing curiosity about and awareness of the prevalence of this illness. It is critical to know how someone struggling with disordered eating or an eating disorder is affected by it. We hope this book will also correct some misconceptions about this common but also detrimental illness. We are also personally invested in addressing eating disorders and want to share a little about our motivation.

FROM JESSICA D. BARTLEY, PSYD, LCSW, CMPC

Jessica was baffled as she watched her college roommate struggle with an eating disorder. When Jessica reached out to her roommate's parents for help, they told her that she must be jealous and that nothing was wrong. It was difficult for her to watch helplessly as distance grew between her and her roommate and their friendship deteriorated. As Jessica pursued graduate education in social work and later psychology, she always remained curious about eating disorders. She began working at EDCare Denver as a practicum student and returned there, after training at Ohio State University, to work as a professional. EDCare provided Jessica, a former elite athlete, with the opportunity to create, with her colleague, Dr. Kate Bennett, a program geared toward athletes with eating disorders and merge two professional interests into one.

Jessica is currently a clinical assistant professor in the Graduate School of Professional Psychology and the director of the Center of Performance Excellence (CPEX) at the University of Denver. She also is a member of a private practice, Sport & Performance Excellence Consultants (SPEX), and she continues to work with collegiate, Olympic, and professional athletes on mental health, including eating disorders, as well as performance.

FROM MELISSA G. STRENO, PSYD, CMPC

Throughout the earlier part of her career, Melissa worked solely with clients on sports performance and mental skills training. Repeated experiences of feeling stuck when an athlete presented with possible disordered eating or an eating disorder propelled Melissa to pursue further training and education in order to feel that she could help her athletes more comprehensively. While working to obtain her clinical doctorate, she pursued her passion for helping both current and former athletes work toward recovery from eating disorders. Her experience as a former college athlete and someone who has endured the difficult transition out of sports has added to her authentic desire to provide help in a more effective way to those navigating such difficult transitions.

Melissa is currently a clinical sport psychologist at EDCare, an eating disorder treatment facility in Denver, Colorado. She is also an adjunct professor in sport and performance psychology in the Graduate School of Professional Psychology at the University of Denver and is part of a group private practice focused on sport and performance consulting.

Essential Questions

1. WHAT IS AN EATING DISORDER?

Eating disorders (now referred to clinically as feeding and eating disorders) are characterized by "a persistent disturbance of eating or eating-related behavior that results in altered consumption or absorption of food and significantly impairs physical or psychosocial functioning" (*Diagnostic and Statistical Manual (DSM)*). According to the *Diagnostic and Statistical Manual of Mental Disorders*, fifth edition (*DSM*-5), there are three primary eating disorders: anorexia nervosa (AN), bulimia nervosa (BN), and binge eating disorder (BED). There are also some lesser-known eating disorders in the *DSM*-5 that include pica, rumination, avoidant/restrictive food intake disorder (ARFID), and other specified feeding and eating disorders (OSFED). Also, there are some eating disorders that are not included in the *DSM*-5, such as orthorexia and diabulimia. For more information about what an eating disorder is, see chapter 1.

2. HOW COMMON ARE EATING DISORDERS?

According to the National Eating Disorders Association, more than 70 million individuals, with 30 million of them in the United States alone, struggle with eating disorders. The existence of eating disorders has been more evidently on the rise for many reasons, which will be detailed throughout the text. Additionally, more people are speaking up about their own struggle and the need for support, which has amplified the awareness and recognition of one of the most lethal mental illnesses. Please reference chapter 1 for more specifics about the prevalence of eating disorders.

3. WHO GETS EATING DISORDERS?

It is tough to predict who will get an eating disorder, but there are several contributions to the development of an eating disorder including genetics/biology, family history, temperament/traits, societal view of body image/social media, and trauma. There are also some causes and risk factors that specifically affect minority groups including men, racial and ethnic minorities, sexual minorities, and, very specifically, athletes. Please reference Chapter 3 for more information about causes and risk factors related to eating disorders.

4. WHAT CAUSES AN EATING DISORDER?

Similar to risk factors, there are several causes for the development of an eating disorder, and it is very rare for there to be only one root cause that predisposes a person to fall into this illness. Some of the causes involve genetics, and there are environmental, social, and cultural factors as well. Another common cause for the development of an eating disorder is the need for control. The experience of this need, as well as the behaviors used to obtain a felt sense of control, will vary tremendously from person to person and among the various types of eating disorders. We also know that body dissatisfaction is one of the primary causes and maintaining factors for the development of an eating disorder. Risk factors that typically precede the start of eating disorder (ED) behaviors and often predict the start of clinically significant ED diagnoses are examined in depth throughout chapter 3.

5. WHAT ARE THE SIGNS OR SYMPTOMS OF AN EATING DISORDER?

Signs or symptoms of an eating disorder vary depending on the type of eating disorder but also on where individuals are situated in the progression of their disorder. While many assume that an eating disorder is identifiable from an initial physical impression, such as low weight, brittle hair, or swollen cheeks, there are many other ways to spot the start or progression of this illness, but they are not always visible to the eye. Psychological and emotional shifts, such as increased depression or anxiety, as well as social or behavioral changes, like isolation, can also be red flags that someone is not doing well and needs support. Chapter 4 provides a more comprehensive and detailed explanation of specific symptoms or warning signs present in someone struggling with an eating disorder.

6. WHAT DOES AN EATING DISORDER LOOK LIKE?

There is not one thing that an eating disorder looks like. While an individual diagnosed with binge eating disorder could appear overweight or an individual with AN could appear underweight, appearances do not always reflect the diagnosis. And for this reason, weight has actually been removed as a criterion for all the eating disorders. To learn more about what eating disorders look like, see chapter 4.

7. WHAT ARE THE RISKS OF AN EATING DISORDER?

There are a number of serious risks with eating disorders. There are risks with all the eating disorders, such as an obsession or fixation with food and/or diets as well as abnormal labs (e.g., potassium, sodium, glucose, phosphorus, magnesium, and blood counts that are not within an appropriate range). There are also some risks that are specific to the various disorders. For example, there are more obvious risks for AN such as weight loss, hair loss and lanugo, dry skin, brittle nails, bruising, tearing, and popped blood vessels. There are also less obvious risks such as cold hands and feet, as well as dizziness and exhaustion. For BN, there are often swollen salivary glands that cause swelling in the cheeks or jawline. Purging via vomiting is also observable by cuts on one's fingers and/or hands as well as cavities, sensitive and discolored teeth, and the erosion of tooth enamel. For binge eating disorder, some of the recurrently observed medical symptoms include gastrointestinal problems, abnormal blood pressure levels, high cholesterol, as well as a predisposition to type 2 diabetes. Unfortunately, there are many more risks of eating disorders, and these can be explored further in chapter 3.

8. WHAT TREATMENTS ARE AVAILABLE FOR EATING DISORDERS?

As you will learn in chapter 5, there are various levels of treatments for eating disorders. For outpatient and intensive outpatient treatments, an individual must be medically stable and not need daily medical monitoring. The individual must also be psychiatrically stable and have symptoms under sufficient control to be able to function in normal social, educational, or vocational situations. For treatment in partial hospitalization, an individual is medically stable, but the ED symptoms impair functioning—although there is no immediate risk—and daily assessment of physiologic and mental status is needed. An individual is also psychiatrically stable but is unable to function in normal social, educational, or vocational situations and engages in daily binge eating, purging, fasting or very limited food intake, or other pathogenic weight-control techniques. For residential treatment, an individual is medically stable and requires no intensive medical intervention. An individual is also psychiatrically impaired and unable to respond to partial hospital or outpatient treatment. In inpatient treatment, an individual is medically unstable as determined by unstable or depressed vital signs, laboratory findings presenting acute health risk, and complications due to coexisting medical problems, such as diabetes. The individual is psychiatrically unstable as determined by rapidly worsening symptoms, suicidal, and unable to contract for safety. Inpatient treatment typically requires a period of outpatient follow-up and aftercare to address underlying issues in the individual's eating disorder.

9. ARE THERE ED TREATMENT GROUPS?

There are hundreds of ED treatment groups across the country. There are groups through treatment centers and mental health facilities. University counseling centers often provide support groups for their students on college campuses. There are also organizations that provide access to support groups, including the National Association of Anorexia Nervosa and Associated Disorders (ANAD) and Overeaters Anonymous (OA). The organization Mirror Mirror (mirror-mirror.org) has a support-group structure and allows individuals in communities across the country to utilize its goals and rules to form ED groups. The Eating Disorder Foundation (EDF) has various support groups for individuals struggling with eating disorders, as well as separate support groups for their family and friends. EDF also offers support groups for specialized populations, including men, the gay and lesbian community, and athletes. Virtual support groups are also offered through EDF. Eating Disorder Hope is a great resource for locating support groups throughout the country. For more information on where to locate support groups, see chapter 8.

10. HOW CAN I HELP SOMEONE WHO HAS AN EATING DISORDER?

This question is one of the most difficult to answer because it depends on the individuals struggling, their level of present denial or acceptance, and their willingness to accept help. While they may have the needed resources and support outlets, such as a robust outpatient team or the convenience of strong support groups, not all individuals with an eating disorder are equally ready to accept the help or accountability intended to help them get well. It is important to remember that those in the helping role are not responsible for finding a solution for someone in the trenches of an eating disorder but instead can highlight the available avenues of support, show compassion and patience, and consistently engage in their own self-care. For more specific examples and ideas revolving around helping someone with an eating disorder, please reference chapter 7.

1

What Are Eating Disorders?

According to the National Eating Disorders Association (NEDA), more than 70 million individuals worldwide, with more than 30 million of them in the United States alone, struggle with eating disorders. And we are learning that eating disorders do not discriminate and can impact individuals of all ages, races and ethnicities, genders, sexual orientations, socioeconomic statuses, and ability statuses. Of the 30 million individuals struggling with eating disorders in the United States, 10 million of these individuals are male. Over the past few years, more individuals who identify as racial and ethnic minorities in the United States and across the world are reporting struggles with eating disorders too. According to the Minnesota Adolescent Health Study, "dieting was associated with weight dissatisfaction, perceived overweight, and low body pride in all ethnic groups." Often, when various studies have examined at how eating disorders have emerged, researchers looked at the shifts in population, the demographics of the population, availability of food for the population, and economic stability as well as traditional gender roles and family structure. There has also been recent evidence to support the idea that people have been displaying symptoms of eating disorders for hundreds of years.

Eating disorders (now referred to clinically as feeding and eating disorders) are characterized by "a persistent disturbance of eating or eating-related behavior that results in altered consumption or absorption of food and significantly impairs physical or psychosocial functioning" (*Diagnostic and Statistical Manual of Mental Disorder*, fifth edition (*DSM-5*)).

1

According to the *Diagnostic and Statistical Manual of Mental Disorders,* fifth edition (*DSM-5*), there are three primary eating disorders: anorexia nervosa (AN), bulimia nervosa (BN), and binge eating disorder (BED). There are also some lesser-known eating disorders in the *DSM-5*, including pica, rumination, avoidant/restrictive food intake disorder (ARFID), and other specified feeding and eating disorders (OSFED). This book will focus primarily on anorexia nervosa, bulimia nervosa, and binge eating disorder. There are also eating disorders that are not in the *DSM-5* but will be addressed here; these include orthorexia and diabulimia.

ANOREXIA NERVOSA

Anorexia nervosa, or simply anorexia, is an eating disorder characterized by weight loss. It is important to note the difference between the terms *anorexia* and *anorexia nervosa*. *Anorexia* simply refers to a loss of appetite and can be used to describe a symptom of another disease or illness. *Anorexia nervosa* is the true name of the eating disorder and encompasses a fear of weight gain, negative body image, and contributing mood symptoms that influence a lack of adequate nutritional intake. For simplification purposes, though, we will refer to *anorexia nervosa* as *anorexia* throughout the book. Anorexia can take shape in two forms: the restricting type or the binge eating/purging type. The restricting type is characterized by intaking a limited amount of food due to fasting, excessively exercising, or dieting. The binge eating/purging type is characterized by persistent binge eating behaviors or using compensatory behaviors to control one's weight, such as vomiting or misusing laxatives, diet pills, or diuretics. Commonalities for both types of anorexia include significant fear of weight gain; distress around one's body weight, shape, or size; and a weighing less than one should, based on age, sex, and physical development. Shared physical symptoms of anorexia may include, but are not limited to, low energy, muscle weakness, lower heart rate and body temperature, and emotional characteristics such as isolation, depression, inability to concentrate, and interrupted sleep patterns.

Almost 1 percent of females and 0.3 percent of males in the United States will suffer from anorexia during their lifetime. Various stereotypes associated with eating disorders have contributed to a widespread belief that anorexia only affects females; however, the prevalence of males impacted by anorexia has continued to grow in recent years. In addition, many more individuals battle body dissatisfaction and subclinical disordered eating attitudes and behaviors, with the numbers of males and females being comparable. From what we know, the primary cause for the development of anorexia is body dissatisfaction. Alarmingly, anorexia is also starting to manifest earlier in life for both males and females. The average age for the onset of anorexia used to be 13 to 17 years, but it has dropped to 9 to 12 years due to the increase in children impacted by the disorder, with children as young as 7 years of age diagnosed. Anorexia is a type of eating disorder that currently has the highest mortality rate of all mental health diagnoses. This is due to the physical impact of starving an individual's body and brain and the increased susceptibility to the individual completing suicide. Males are often observed reaching out for support later in the course of their illness, which has elevated the mortality rate for males above females with anorexia. Males make up 25 percent of the population of those struggling with anorexia.

In 2011, Marques and colleagues analyzed results from three large data sets concentrated on prevalence rates of eating disorders among non-Latinx white, Latinx, Asian, and African American men and women. Their study supported similar one-year and lifetime prevalence rates for all the above ethnic minority groups within the United States. However, they did point out distinctions between ethnic groups for each individual type of eating disorder that will be included throughout this chapter. Consistent with earlier studies supporting the notion of low anorexia prevalence rates among Asians, Latinx, and African Americans, researchers have not found any difference in prevalence rates of anorexia across these major ethnic groups within the United States.

BULIMIA NERVOSA

Bulimia nervosa, or simply bulimia, has comparable prevalence rates for females (1% to 1.5% according to *DSM*-5) and is characterized by frequent episodes of consuming very large amounts of food in a limited amount of time (e.g., two hours). This behavior is followed by attempts to compensate for weight gain, such as self-induced vomiting, laxative and diuretic misuse, fasting, and excessive exercise. These episodes are also accompanied by a feeling of being out of control. The severity of bulimia can range from mild to moderate to severe based on the average number of compensatory behaviors in a given week. The average onset of bulimia is 20 years of age, with onset before puberty and after 40 being uncommon. Unfortunately, bulimia is on the rise. Dissimilar to anorexia, death from bulimia is rare, but it is possible due to imbalances with fluids and/or electrolytes, tears in the esophagus, gastric ruptures, and heart arrhythmia. In the same way anorexia is not limited to females, the prevalence rate for males who will develop bulimia is 0.1 to 0.5 percent. Marques and colleagues' study found that a lifetime prevalence of bulimia is significantly greater among Latinx and African Americans. Citing a previous study within their work, they also reported lower occurrences of anorexia and bulimia among Asian Americans compared to the general population.

BINGE EATING DISORDER

Binge eating disorder (BED) is the newest addition to the *DSM* and is characterized by eating more food than usual in a finite amount of time—for example, two hours—and eating more rapidly than usual, eating until physically uncomfortable, eating when not hungry, and eating alone often due to guilt and shame or feeling guilty and/or shameful after these episodes. Similar to bulimia, the severity of BED can range from mild to moderate to severe based on the average number of binges each week. While BED is the newest addition to the *DSM*, it is actually the most common eating disorder, with an estimated 2.8 million people meeting criteria for the diagnosis. That is three times the number of people diagnosed with anorexia and bulimia combined. BED often begins in the late adolescence or early adulthood although it is most common for women in early adulthood and men in middle adulthood. Marques et al., found an increase in the prevalence of binge eating behaviors within the Latinx, Asian, and African American population compared to non-Latinx white groups. While looking specifically at adolescents, NEDA also confirmed the presence of binge eating disorder to be more common among all minority groups.

With regard to the medical consequences of BED, clinical obesity, diabetes, and repetitive weight gains and losses—the latter also referred to as yo-yo dieting—are common physical outcomes. These can all disrupt sleep, interfere with one's metabolism and digestion, and contribute to abnormal blood pressure readings. The social stigma of being a certain size can also be a psychologically devastating effect of BED. Additionally, it can contribute to difficulty concentrating and obsessions around food.

PICA

Pica is the persistent eating of nonnutritive or nonfood substances (e.g., tissues or cotton balls, glass, chalk or crayons) that is inconsistent with the developmental age, culture, or religion of the individual. Pica tends to be more common among children with developmental disabilities or children between the ages of two and three. There are significant health consequences with pica because nonnutritive and nonfood substances can cause obstructions or perforate the esophagus, stomach, bowels, or intestines as well as cause infections in or poison the body. While this is one of the diagnosable feeding and eating disorders, it is not reported often and is not one of the primary eating disorders addressed in the book.

RUMINATION

Another eating disorder that is diagnosable with the most recent manual and often accompanies other eating disorders is rumination. Rumination is the repeated regurgitation (e.g., rechewing, swallowing, reswallowing, and spitting out) of food. The average age of onset is usually between 3 and 12 months, and it can be fatal in infancy. Again, this disorder is not reported often and is not one of the primary eating disorders addressed in the book.

AVOIDANT/RESTRICTIVE FOOD INTAKE DISORDER

The last diagnosable eating disorder is avoidant/restrictive food intake disorder (ARFID), previously selective eating disorder (SED). ARFID is the inability to meet appropriate nutritional and/or energy needs and is associated with significant weight loss, significant nutritional deficiency, or dependence on nutritional supplements. The ARFID diagnosis is often reserved for individuals who do not meet the criteria for anorexia but still experience clinically significant struggles with eating and food. As a result of struggling with eating and food, the individual is not able to consume an appropriate amount of food and may end up losing weight. An individual might also avoid eating certain colors (e.g., green) or textures (e.g., yogurt or applesauce), might have difficulty digesting specific foods, or might be afraid to eat certain foods after a traumatic episode of choking or vomiting. Finally, an individual might only eat small portions or have no appetite altogether. The individual may also have problems at school or work due to issues with food and eating. For example, the person might not attend a working lunch or complete work on time because of the time it takes to eat. It is important to note that these issues with food and eating are not related to a lack of food or "food insecurity" (e.g., issues of children living in poverty). As ARFID is a relatively new diagnosis, there is little information available on the development of this eating disorder or its prognosis except that symptoms typically show up in infancy or childhood but can continue into adulthood. Unfortunately, many individuals with ARFID go on to develop another eating disorder such as anorexia or bulimia, which is another reason that development and prognosis are not clear.

OTHER SPECIFIED FEEDING OR EATING DISORDERS

Other specified feeding or eating disorders (OSFED) replaced eating disorders not otherwise specified in the *DSM*. They have symptoms or characteristics of feeding or eating disorders but do not meet criteria for the other feeding or eating disorders—often due to time constraints. Some of these eating disorders are bulimia nervosa (of low frequency and/or limited duration), binge eating disorder (of low frequency and/or limited duration), and atypical anorexia nervosa. There are also night eating syndrome, episodes of eating at night, and purging disorder, regular purging but in the absence of binge eating. OSFED is sometimes misinterpreted as a subclinical diagnosis or a less serious eating disorder, but it is not. In the past, studies have shown that individuals who were diagnosed with OSFED experience ED symptoms that are just as, if not more, severe than individuals who received a formal anorexia or bulimia diagnosis. Furthermore, Le Grange and colleagues found that three-quarters of individuals diagnosed with OSFED had other mental health diagnoses, and more than a quarter of individuals endorsed suicidality. Only about 30 percent of individuals who seek treatment are diagnosed with OSFED. The reasons for developing OSFED will differ from person to person. Some of the causes involve genetic as well as environmental, social, and cultural factors.

Night Eating Syndrome

One of the more common diagnoses addressed under OSFED is night eating syndrome. Night eating syndrome is often mistaken for binge eating disorder. While an individual diagnosed with night eating syndrome often binges, the activity is different from binge eating because the food is consumed at night and is not necessarily a binge, and the loss of control over food is not necessarily there. However, there is tremendous guilt and shame around eating at night. According to the National Institute of Mental Health (NIMH), it is estimated that 1.5 percent of the population struggles with night eating syndrome and just as many men as women struggle.

An individual with night eating syndrome is likely obese or overweight and will also struggle with health problems associated with being obese or overweight, including, but not limited to, high cholesterol and blood pressure in addition to diabetes. An individual who struggles with obesity is also at an increased risk of heart and gall bladder diseases as well as several types of cancer. An individual with night eating syndrome will often have a history of substance abuse and may also struggle with depression. Most individuals with night eating syndrome who struggle with depression tend to be more depressed at night and will also report struggling with clinical sleep disorders.

The specific causes of night eating syndrome are unknown, but there are typically a number of contributing factors. For example, teenagers and young adults often develop poor habits of eating late and are unable to break the habit when they become adults working regular business hours. Working through lunch and dieting could also be considered contributing factors. When calories are restricted during the day, the common response is to compensate or even overcompensate at night.

ORTHOREXIA NERVOSA

There are two other eating disorders that are not a part of the *DSM-5* but have become more prevalent. Orthorexia nervosa is an eating disorder that includes an obsession with a healthy—possibly perfect—diet to an extent that clearly hinders everyday functioning. For example, an individual diagnosed with orthorexia might avoid artificial colors, flavors, or preservatives; pesticides or genetic modifications; fat, sugar, or salt; animal or dairy products; and other seemingly unhealthy ingredients in food. *Orthorexia* was a term coined by Steven Bratman, MD, for patients who were overly health-obsessed.

Although orthorexia nervosa first appeared in the literature in 1997, the standard criteria for the eating disorder have been around for much longer. According to research from the University of Maryland/Sheppard Pratt Psychiatry Residency Program, "society is faced with updates on the latest food diet, warnings about certain foods and products, and an ever-changing set of guidelines on how to live a healthier life and in this complicated cultural environment, many individuals find it difficult to not worry about their eating habits."

According to NEDA, "food inflexibility can lead to guilt or self-loathing if a 'bad' food is consumed, as well as anxiety about food planning and isolation from social events with food and drinks. It can also cause nutritional deficiencies when entire food groups are removed from a person's diet."

Orthorexia can take many forms. It can include compulsively checking nutrition labels or only consuming seemingly pure and organic foods. It can also be an obsession with fitness experts or healthy lifestyle bloggers or an overwhelming interest in what others are eating. Merely checking a label or following a fitness expert would not be considered orthorexia, but the obsession with these does indicate the disorder.

Since orthorexia is not a well-documented or well-researched eating disorder, there are not reliable statistics on its prevalence. Unfortunately, it is clear that thought patterns and behaviors evident in orthorexia often lead individuals into other eating disorders.

DIABULIMIA

Diabulimia was first documented in the literature in the late 1980s, but it has only recently been covered in popular press. Diabulimia is an eating disorder associated with people diagnosed with type 1 diabetes who deliberately give themselves less insulin than needed, for the purpose of weight loss. According to NEDA, diabulimia has some of the most significant health consequences: inability to concentrate, high cholesterol, high glucose levels, glucose in the urine, diabetic ketoacidosis (i.e., unsafe levels of ketones in the blood), exhaustion, unquenchable thirst and severe dehydration, muscle loss, bacterial skin infections, staph infections, yeast infections, menstrual disruption, retinopathy, neuropathy, peripheral arterial disease, atherosclerosis (i.e., a fattening of the arterial walls), steatohepatitis (i.e., a type of liver disease), stroke, coma, and even death. Death is actually three times more likely if an individual with diabetes manipulates insulin for the purpose of weight loss. With regard to the prevalence of diabulimia, 38 percent of females and 16 percent of males who have type 1 diabetes presumably struggle with diabulimia.

As explained above, eating disorders are very complicated illnesses that can impact people from all walks of life. In the coming chapters, we will go into much more detail about the causes, symptoms, and available treatments for each of the described eating disorders. Additionally, we will talk about the impact an eating disorder has on other realms of one's life and on one's support system. We know that social media and societal influences have created significant issues around the development and continuation of eating disorders. Discussion about ways to confront these obstacles and triggers will be included as well.

2

The History of Eating Disorders

Understanding the history of eating disorders can be a useful tool before diving into learning more about the complexities, specific symptoms, and effects of each type. There have been significant changes regarding diagnostic procedures, conceptualizations, and treatments of eating disorders for hundreds of years, which makes this chapter quite comprehensive and detailed. This chapter will outline the main contributors who first identified signs and symptoms of what we now know as eating disorders and how this body of knowledge has evolved alongside the medical field in general and the classification system of psychiatric illnesses.

FIRST CONCEPTUALIZATIONS OF EATING DISORDERS

Many people assume Richard Morton's narrative on anorexia in 1689 was the first to highlight and describe the behaviors of eating disorders. However, there are even earlier accounts dating back to the medieval times, between the 12th and 15th centuries. This was during a time when women starved themselves to honor and express their spirituality and holiness. Catherine of Siena was one of the most well-known saints who engaged in fasting for religious reasons during what was described as the start of a starvation "outbreak." Her story of personal loss, sacrifice and devotion to God, and eventual death because of restricting her intake prompted multiple female followers to pass away from fasting.

Whether that symptom of fasting or restricting, which was then called *anorexia mirabilis* or "miraculously inspired loss of appetite," has the same origin as modern anorexia is unknown. However, anorexia mirabilis has contributed to our understanding of eating disorders, specifically the social and cultural associations that impact an individual's relationship with food. While the shared goal of achieving perfection or being seen in a particular way by others has prevailed since the 13th century, the specific motives have changed over time. For example, women in the medieval period manipulated their food for religious reasons and a desire to be viewed in a positive light by God. Over time, this motive shifted to goals involving socioeconomic relations and, eventually, to a more modern attempt to achieve society's definition of a perfect body weight, shape, or size. Researchers warn against drawing any similarities between anorexia mirabilis and modern anorexia besides the biological parallels.

While more primitive and subjective, one story that stood out among many physicians and members of the Royal Society involved an English girl named Martha Taylor. Martha was 19 years old when she began a fast that lasted more than 13 months. Reportedly, her period of restriction was caused by various medical incidents that resulted in depression and isolation. This was one of the very first documented cases of someone surviving while intentionally limiting food and liquid intake and suffering destructive physical complications. Despite numerous visitors wanting to see this Martha in person and various philosophers, theorists, and physicians sharing her story among themselves, most people did not trust this presentation (display of symptoms) as an honest account of her experience. Many also did not attribute her behaviors to a psychiatric cause. Some aspects of Martha's disease paralleled the present-day diagnosis of an eating disorder. However, it was not until 1689, when Richard Morton's paper on "nervous consumption" was published, that issues such as Martha's were viewed as actual eating disorders.

Richard Morton is known as one of the first individuals to put a name to the condition we now define as anorexia nervosa (AN). When describing restriction as "nervous consumption," or "consumption proceeding from melancholy," he attributed the cause of the behaviors to mood shifts, specifically depression and anxiety. Morton referred to these as "passions of the mind." He ruled out any previous underlying medical cause or disease and encouraged individuals suffering to include variety in their diet, avoid isolation, and seek help as early as possible. All these recommendations moderately align with current treatment methods. Morton's text, which highlighted the origin, symptoms, prognosis, and treatment of anorexia, was favorably considered as a medical textbook for many years.

There was also exploration into the mid-16th-century phenomenon of what was called the "green sickness" or chlorosis. The English said this occurred during a female's transition from puberty to sexual maturity. Symptoms included loss of appetite, amenorrhea, and mood changes. Researchers have since studied the connections and similarities between this Renaissance-era disease and what we know today as anorexia. While the terminology used to explain the sources of green sickness and anorexia was different, the identified risk factors and causes to both illnesses overlapped even among different social classes within the 16th century. As time progressed and green sickness became more widespread, treatment for the symptoms occurring during this maturity period also became more comprehensive. Diet changes, exercise, bloodletting, which referred to withdrawing blood from a person, and fragrant potions were all encouraged. The intention was to restore balance to the uterus, the organ believed to be the main culprit of illness in women.

Exploring content from 17th century plays portraying the overwhelming experiences of adolescent girls, researchers have looked closely at material illustrating an anorexic body type. Evidence points to the belief that restriction of food, which led to what was described as green sickness, was used as a means to avoid sexual maturity and other expected milestones, such as marriage or childbirth. By avoiding these life phases, the belief was that one would remain pure. This parallels one of many common modern functions of an eating disorder, which is to stall and avoid physical maturity and independence by using restriction and other eating-disorder behaviors.

The phenomenon of fasting became a focus of investigation throughout the 17th and 18th centuries. More attention was fixed on observing those enduring a fast, and assessing how long a human body could go without food. These individuals were no longer just viewed as seeking sainthood but possibly suffering from a physical or mental sickness. Due to the availability of print resources and the word spreading about the growing number of cases, individuals from all social and religious classes began experimenting with starvation behaviors.

As more knowledge and information of those in a malnourished state became available, there were also advancements in assessing those who were struggling. This information became available to 19th-century clinicians as part of a disease classification system. In fact, the term *anorexia mirabilis* was included in medical texts during this time period. However, due to continued conflict and the inability to distinguish between anorexia mirabilis and anorexia, the term *fasting girls* was used instead to describe females engaging in extended periods of food restriction.

During this time period, the corset became another contributor toward achieving a particular body shape and size. A corset was an article of clothing designed to help shape a woman's body into a thinner figure. Despite the discomfort and physically damaging effects of wearing a corset, many women wore one daily throughout the 19th century. This was only the start of an excessive number of inventions, fad diets, and merchandise aimed at achieving a specific body image for years to come.

EARLY RESEARCHERS AND PRACTITIONERS OF EATING DISORDERS

In the late 19th century, anorexia became categorized as a new disease rather than a symptom caused by religious beliefs. During this time, it was also a common sign of many other diseases with deteriorating qualities. Eventually, though, it came to stand on its own rather than being classified as a widespread medical symptom that merely described someone refusing to eat. While it was still defined in medical dictionaries as a lack of appetite, doctors began to hold more power than clergy members. As a result, they began challenging previous reports that this illness was not caused by mental factors. This shift also paralleled more comprehensive changes within the medical field. Diseases were now starting to become more distinguished from one another, with new names and a more complex classification system.

As described earlier in the chapter, there was plenty of evidence early on that particular sociocultural components could contribute to the development of an eating disorder. Many people wrote about and studied the development of anorexia, especially among younger females, throughout these years. However, Sir William Withey Gull of London, England, and Dr. Ernest-Charles Lasègue of Paris, France, have been described as the pioneers in defining anorexia as a full-scale illness. Around 1873, they also brought it closer to within the scope of science and medicine. Gull labeled the presentation "anorexia nervosa" and described the physical attributes that accompanied this illness. Charles termed it "anorexia hysterique" and began to explain the additional psychological contributions. A French physician by the name of Louis-Victor Marcé also added to the growing definitions of anorexia from a more thorough medical standpoint. His statement to the Société Médico-Psychologique (medico-psychological society) of Paris in 1859 outlined specific symptoms among his cases, such as refusal to eat and fixation on food. Marcé also recommended the involvement of family members during treatment in order to prevent relapse. Some say that Marcé's contributions were actually presented prior to Gull's and Lasègue's, and that those men did not give him credit in their clinical interpretations. As these earlier forerunners revealed their work, other doctors responded to these articles and began reporting similar presentations in their own patients, some even witnessing similar symptoms in males. At one point between 1920 and 1940, there was the belief that this presentation was actually the effect of a pituitary dysfunction. But further investigation and comparison of symptoms confirmed that it was not pituitary-related.

Late in the 19th century, Gull, Morton, and Lasègue all agreed on the clinical criteria for anorexia. The five main components at this time included occurrence in young girls and young women, decreased intake of food, thinness (resulting from decreased intake), physical restlessness, and a lack of physical explanation for one's symptoms. All these would indicate psychological origin, which contributed to a lack of insight and resistance to treatment. But as more people joined the conversation around distinguishing anorexia from other medical diseases, the belief that it was more psychological grew.

Within their case studies, both Morton and Gull had mentioned the existence of males with anorexia; however, more consistent evidence and interest did not surface until much later. Specific criteria that excluded males, such as amenorrhea as well as stereotypes within society, were established early on for anorexia, so the perception that males could also struggle with the disease was not recognized publicly until the late 1960s and early 1970s. The study of males having anorexia has steadily increased since the latter part of the 20th century.

In 1973, Hilde Bruch, a German-born American doctor and psychoanalyst, released her first book, titled *Eating Disorders: Obesity, Anorexia Nervosa, and the Person*. Bruch had spent years exploring and researching within the field of childhood obesity but was considered an innovator when it came to releasing material specifically focusing on anorexia. Five years later, her most popular publication, *The Golden Cage: The Enigma of Anorexia Nervosa*, prompted a significant shift in awareness around the prevalence of anorexia. This was especially true for those outside the medical field. Bruch wrote about the influence of an adolescent individual's perception of weakness and distorted body image on lower levels of self-esteem and increased levels of compliance. Her work emphasized the power one works to grasp by feeling in control of her body during periods of unfamiliar transition and development. She also highlighted the way in which ED behaviors slow the progression of independence. Many see her contributions as influential in approaching eating disorders as serious medical illnesses. As the 20th century progressed, Bruch and other researchers and physicians, including British psychiatrist Gerald Russell, shared their observations after following individuals over many decades. Russell noted a shift in how the symptoms of anorexia have transformed from a fear of maturation and independence to the fixation on physical appearance and fear of becoming fat. This also paralleled a change in anorexics' growing level of commitment to their illness. Bruch added her opinion on the difference between anorexics who came up with their symptoms individually and those who decades later seemed to copy others' symptoms in order to be seen. This created a great amount of comparison among those struggling with an eating disorder. It is another example of why there was confusion early on when defining and diagnosing anorexia, as well as bulimia.

There is documentation, often of Greek or Latin origin, of the term *bulimia* dating back to the 15th century. While multiple variations of the term were referenced in medical texts, it most often signified an intense hunger followed by vomiting. Researchers and historians have spent time documenting cases that covered 300 years and were composed of both females and males with varying backgrounds. Some cases were directly linked to more a bizarre phenomenon, such as worms in the intestines, while others were said to have been caused by digestive abnormalities. The lack of certainty only caused greater confusion. Some of the most extreme documented cases went as far as including individuals who ate small animals in response to their powerful hunger. Physicians and writers began publishing their own accounts of different types of bulimia and treatment methods, often distinguished by variations in specific physical symptoms and the presence of vomiting.

In 1702, Stephen Blanchard, a Dutch physician, shared his view on bulimia. He explained that bulimic behaviors were used to provide oneself temporary relief during a negative mood state.

Around 1974, there was an increased focus on surfacing bulimic symptoms in patients. There was also speculation that these behaviors were occurring much earlier. Bruch was again a contributor to these observations when she noticed some of her own patients vomiting food in order to avoid weight gain. While bulimic criteria also included a significant fear of weight gain, it soon became categorized by itself, mainly due to its most identifiable characteristics of overeating and self-provoked vomiting. The progression of its inclusion as a separate diagnosis will be discussed later in this chapter.

With regard to long-term steadiness of this illness, researchers Fichter and Quadflieg followed 311 females for 12 years. All these individuals were given various ED diagnoses. The researchers found anorexia to be the most stable diagnosis over time. Binge eating disorder was shown to have the greatest variability in symptom presentation, but it also overlapped with the criteria for bulimia. The similar symptom appearance between bulimia and binge eating was said to have been due to related biological and psychological characteristics that contribute to the continuation of both illnesses.

RECOGNITION OF EATING DISORDERS BY THE MEDICAL FIELD

In the 1950s and 1960s, anorexia was often treated with antipsychotic drugs. Later in the second half of the century, psychotherapy was added to the list of treatment options, and medications were rarely the only form of intervention. During this time, family therapy, as well various techniques from different theoretical orientations, such as cognitive behavioral therapy, contributed to the expansion in treatment approaches.

Unfortunately, there has been a significant lack of training in the assessment and treatment of eating disorders within medical school curricula. The shortage has been described as quite surprising and appalling, based on the significant need to assess and treat the psychiatric disorder with the highest mortality rate. The lack of experience and training opportunities for medical students have been well documented in various studies looking at a variety of areas within medicine, including general psychiatry, child and adolescent medicine, family medicine, internal medicine, and pediatrics, to name a few.

With the intention of identifying gaps and needs in medical school curricula, Pennsylvania State University is one example of an institution that led a study analyzing the training experiences related to eating disorders within residency programs. Surveys from 637 training coordinators revealed a significant deficiency in available education, with some rotations only lasting less than a month. Even more surprisingly, some residents have only received a few hours of training in eating disorders. Contributors toward a lack of ED training opportunities include variation in geographic settings, availability of few suitable experts to lead the trainings, and an absence of overall standards specific to all medical students. In 2014, Girz and colleagues documented an even larger study involving 17 Canadian residency programs that concentrated on child and adolescent eating disorders. This study included 880 participants from multiple disciplines within medicine. Utilizing similar methods to the study described above, the purpose was to collect data about the level of competence in treating eating disorders and the actual amount and intensity of training provided. Additionally, they looked at the association between the amount of education received and the medical students' perceptions of acquired knowledge about eating disorders. Likewise, findings revealed that more than 70 percent of participants admitted receiving less than five hours of training directly related to this illness, and the areas of pediatrics and psychiatry reported the greatest exposure. Most of the respondents were in their first year of medical school, which would indicate less opportunity for this training to have taken place. However, even those in their fourth year conveyed an insufficient amount of education. Results also revealed increased comfort and competence in treating anorexia compared to other types of eating disorders among children and adolescents. These specific findings from both studies have prompted a more direct push for the inclusion of online training, shared training experiences among various medical specialties, the inclusion of best practices for assessing and treating eating disorders, and additional education focusing on evidence-based treatment for eating disorders.

PUBLIC AND CULTURAL AWARENESS OF EATING DISORDERS

We are increasingly hearing about celebrities and famous icons who have or are currently struggling with an eating disorder. However, this is not a new phenomenon. In hindsight, many actors, singers, artists within the Hollywood scene and public eye fought ED behaviors long before it was even considered a psychiatric illness or included in the *Diagnostic and Statistical Manual of Mental Disorders* (*DSM*). For example, there is speculation that both Judy Garland and Audrey Hepburn struggled with their weight as a result of pressure to be thin in order to maintain popularity within their careers.

Many believe that it was not until Karen Carpenter's death in the 1980s that the name *anorexia* took on a more significant and influential meaning. Karen Carpenter, lead singer of the band the Carpenters, died in 1983 at the age of 32 due to cardiac complications related to her eating disorder. It has been said that her low self-esteem and striving for control, with regard to both her music career and her relationship with her mother, contributed to the start of her eating disorder. From high school graduation into her short-lived music career, comments about her body image and accolades for intentional weight loss started a snowball effect of physical damage. While friends, family, and fans voiced questions and concerns, a general lack of knowledge about eating disorders led to incorrect assumptions about her recognizable physical changes. Even doctors attributed her symptoms and presentation to anxiety and exhaustion from her lifestyle as a traveling musician. Her battle with anorexia also included the use of ipecac, a drug used to make purging easier. This initiated a ban by the Food and Drug Administration (FDA) on specific over-the-counter laxatives and drugs used to prompt vomiting. Carpenter's struggle with an eating disorder, followed by that of many others, including Princess Diana of Wales, Elton John, and Jane Fonda, was one of the first viewed in the public eye. It contributed to increased attention and concern around this lethal disease and encouraged those who had kept their illness a secret to come forward and seek help.

MILESTONES IN DIAGNOSIS AND TREATMENT

The task of classifying an eating disorder has been a challenge since anorexia was first included in the *DSM*-I. ED symptoms come about and present in a variety of ways, which makes it difficult to include all under one specific diagnosis or label. The criteria used to categorize anorexia in the *DSM*-I and II were often based on unreliable assumptions and stories rather than more currently reliable data and theoretical conceptualizations.

The initial attempt at classifying mental illness occurred in 1840. This involved gathering statistical data by documenting the frequency of "idiocy/insanity." This process lasted until 1880 but produced seven categories, none of which specifically related to an eating disorder. In 1921, the newly named American Psychological Association (APA) worked in conjunction with the New York Academy of Medicine to expand the classification structure for psychiatric disorders. Their work focused mainly on serious psychiatric and neurological disorders. This organization system became part of the first edition of the American Medical Association's *Standard Classified Nomenclature of Disease*. In 1948, the joint efforts of the World Health Organization (WHO) and the US Army added a segment within the sixth revision of the *International Classification of Diseases* (*ICD*) with a focus on mental disorders for the first time ever. The APA committee looked over the *ICD*-6 and put together the first version of the *Diagnostic and Statistical Manual of Mental Disorders* in 1952. Compiled by the APA, the *DSM* serves as a platform for mental health clinicians and helps them to form diagnoses and structure treatment options. It is used for both clinical and research purposes but has undergone multiple revisions and editions since its initial release, similar to the development and organization around the various types of eating disorders.

Anorexia was included in the *DSM*-I in 1952. With improvements in diagnosis, the *DSM*-II was released in 1968. Anorexia was included in this version as a special symptom under the category of feeding disturbances.

DSM-III, which was released at the same time as another revised version of the *ICD*, included what was described as a multiaxial system. Within this edition, there was an intention to provide more precise and valid diagnostic measures for clinicians and research purposes. The debut of *DSM*-III included a new section for eating disorders under the category of disorders of childhood or adolescence. This section included anorexia nervosa, rumination disorder, and pica. Rumination disorder was described as the act of regurgitating food, while pica was defined as repetitively eating food with no nutritional value, such as paint, dirt, or plaster.

The term *bulimia* was referenced in the *DSM*-III. However, its lone criterion was the occurrence of binge eating. Ongoing revisions and awareness of inconsistencies within the developing *DSM* system led to the release of a revised form called the *DSM*-III-R in 1987, in which bulimia nervosa was listed for the first time. This revision also included a more specific set of criteria for bulimia, which closely aligned with the contents of Russell's paper in 1979.

With the incorporation of bulimia as its own disorder rather than a symptom of others, many began to question the distinctions between anorexia and bulimia. Specifically, questions arose regarding the one distinguishing criterion related to weight. Other distinctions between the two included bingeing and purging by means of vomiting, as well as the use of laxatives and/or diuretics. At that point in time, persons diagnosed with anorexia had to be less than 15 percent of their normal weight, but that was not the case for bulimia.

As more specific diagnostic criteria were established when bulimia made its presence, it became clearer that earlier accounts may not have met the full diagnostic criteria. Instead, these were likely only symptoms of bulimia present long before its inclusion in the *DSM*-III. As reported rates of bulimic symptoms became more common, bulimia became difficult to accurately identify due to the variation of individuals being studied. Some were from the community and others were within hospital populations. Additionally, the wide-ranging criteria and vague overlapping symptoms with anorexia continued to pose diagnostic challenges specifically within the *DSM*-III.

A need for more generally shared language related to bulimia contributed to changes within *DSM*-IV. Now that it was more aligned with the developing *ICD* system, the *DSM*-IV was released in 1994. This version included three types of eating disorders. The first was anorexia nervosa, which included two subtypes: restricting and binge/purge type. The next was bulimia nervosa, with two subtypes: purge and non-purge. The third type was eating disorder not otherwise specified, or what has been commonly referred to as EDNOS. This was the term used to describe an eating disorder that did not fall into the category of the other two. The criteria for EDNOS were less exhaustive and specific in relation to the other types of eating disorders; however, EDNOS was most frequently assigned to someone struggling with an eating disorder, especially in outpatient settings. One of the biggest criticisms toward the generalizability of EDNOS was the lack of research. This contributed to less knowledge available to support the best course of treatment for this diagnosis. In order to meet criteria for EDNOS, there had to be significant clinical evidence an eating disorder existed. Additionally, criteria for anorexia and bulimia had to have been ruled out. Renowned psychiatrist Albert Stunkard first spoke of binge eating symptoms early in 1959; however, these symptoms were not included in the *DSM* until 1987, when they were listed as a potential component of a bulimic presentation. Due to many individuals classified in the EDNOS category who were struggling with binge eating behaviors, there was a strong push to replace EDNOS with this diagnosis in the next *DSM* revision.

A revised version of *DSM*-IV, titled the *DSM*-IV-TR, recommended further investigation into binge eating disorder. This disorder was described as overeating to the point of extreme discomfort and feeling out of control. Distinct from bulimia, binge eating disorder did not include any form of compensatory behavior, such as vomiting or laxatives, and was often associated with signs of obesity. *DSM*-IV-TR also advised further exploration around night eating syndrome. This condition was characterized by little food intake throughout the day due to shame or guilt from the previous night's eating episode. While the quantity of food varies among individuals struggling with night eating, the majority of their consumption occurs during the night. Similar to binge eating disorder, a loss of control and secrecy are often associated with this illness.

There was initial controversy in adding binge eating disorder to the *DSM* due to difficulty separating binge eating behaviors and overeating habits. Many of the originally reported cases did not include compensatory behaviors, absence of control over the behaviors, or concern around one's body size or weight. All these characteristics, in addition to the eating of a significant quantity of food in a short amount of time, are representative of modern presentations of bulimia.

Between the years of 2000 and 2007, researchers came back together to study gaps within the literature regarding variations among disorders, including the different types of eating disorders. The end product was various documents and journal articles highlighting areas the researchers felt were in need of closer examination in order to not only make the process of diagnosis and treatment better but also to better align with current psychiatric research. In order to prepare for the release of the next *DSM*, a *DSM* task force was formed to make the recommended changes. The task force completed the most recent version, *DSM*-5, which was released in 2013.

Within this edition of the *DSM*, one of the most significant changes was binge eating disorder's own grouping, which landed within the section on Feeding and Eating Disorders. Throughout further investigation of case studies, it became clear that those previously given the diagnosis of EDNOS were suffering from binge eating behaviors and would benefit from a more accurate identification. This would also help to create individualized treatment plans. Revisions for anorexia and bulimia were also included in the *DSM*-5, specifically the removal of amenorrhea as a criterion for those with anorexia. The term Other Specified Feeding and Eating Disorder (OSFED) was utilized to account for those whose symptoms reflected an eating disorder that contributed to distress, but did not fulfill full criteria for one of the specific diagnoses listed above. Pica, rumination, and avoidant/restrictive food intake disorder were also now classified in the feeding and eating disorders section within the most current version of the *DSM* instead of listed under "Disorders Usually First Diagnosed in Infancy, Childhood, or Adolescence." Further explanation and analysis of the changes within the *DSM*-5 will be included later in the text.

As you can see, the history of eating disorders spans a significant amount of time and involves many influential clinicians, researchers, and physicians in the field. Without this thorough investigation and analysis early on, we would be without the important tools to help treat this devastating illness. Luckily, the interest and resulting contributions have only grown, which has helped provide important information about eating disorders that you will learn about in the upcoming chapters.

3

Causes and Risk Factors

There are numerous risk factors related to the development of an eating disorder. Risk factors tend to come before disordered eating and will often predict the development of an eating disorder. Risk factors do not necessarily cause eating disorders, but they can be contributing factors in the development of an eating disorder. Some risk factors can predict the development of an eating disorder while other risk factors are associated with the actual development of an eating disorder.

CONTRIBUTIONS TO THE DEVELOPMENT OF EATING DISORDERS

Genetics/Biology

There is evidence that eating disorders are potentially rooted in genetics and biology. It has been shown that the genetic and biological influences are not simply due to a single gene but are the results of interactions between multiple genes.

In some individuals with eating disorders, chemicals in the brain that control hunger, appetite, and digestion have been reported to look differently than in brains of individuals without eating disorders. The exact meaning and implications of these differences are still being explored. Additionally, brain-imaging studies have shown that people with eating disorders may have altered brain circuitry that contributes to eating disorders. Differences in the anterior insula and ventral striatal pathways as well as the striatal regions have been discovered. Differences with the serotonin pathway are also being explored. These differences may help to illuminate why people who develop AN are able to restrict, why people who develop BED are vulnerable to bingeing, and why people who develop BN have less control around compensatory behaviors. We will be discussing neurobiology and brain research more in chapter 10.

Also related to biology and genetics, there have been more studies around twins that have provided evidence around the genetic and biological contributions to the development of eating disorders. Simply stated, it is believed that individuals who are born with certain genotypes are at an increased risk for the development of an eating disorder. It has also been confirmed that eating disorders are heritable. According to the Center for Eating Disorders, individuals who have had a family member with an eating disorder are 7 to 12 times more likely to develop one themselves. Newer research is exploring a possible epigenetic influence on ED development. We will discuss genetic factors underlying eating disorders more in chapter 10.

Family History

Historically, parents were typically blamed for their child's eating disorder. As more research is introduced on the various contributing factors, it has become more and more clear that this is not the case. While chaotic family situations might maintain or even exacerbate an eating disorder, it is now understood that families do not cause eating disorders. It is also important to recognize that some family situations, assumed to be contributing factors to an eating disorder, may have developed as a response to a member of the family struggling with their eating disorder. The Academy for Eating Disorders (AED) released a position paper that clarifies the role of the family in the acquisition of eating disorders. The paper points out that there is "no data to support the idea that eating disorders are caused by a certain type of family dynamic or parenting style. Alternatively, there is strong evidence families play an integral role in the recovery process." As we will discuss more in chapter 5, family-based treatment and professionally guided family interventions for younger patients that are implemented early on in the treatment for the eating disorder lead to positive results and improvements.

Temperament/Traits

Several genes associated with specific personality traits have been identified as contributors to eating disorders. Some studies have even correlated aspects of these personality traits with changes in serotonin and dopamine. These aspects of personality are often believed to be inherited and are present long before the onset of an eating disorder as well as during the recovery from an eating disorder. The following traits are common among people who develop an eating disorder, but it is important to note that these personality characteristics can exist in the absence of an eating disorder. The traits are:

- obsessive thinking
- harm avoidance
- neuroticism
- impulsivity, especially in BN
- rigidity and excessive persistence, especially in AN

Researchers at King's College London identified a set of five obsessive-compulsive personality traits including "perfectionism, inflexibility, rule driven, drive-for-order and symmetry, excessive doubt, and cautiousness and found that women with AN and BN were significantly more likely to have shown signs of these in childhood." On the contrary, these personality traits were rarely seen in individuals without eating disorders. In addition, it was 7 times more likely that individuals with these personality traits would develop an eating disorder and 35 times more likely for an individual with all 5 of these traits to develop an eating disorder.

Aside from other obsessive-compulsive traits, individuals with eating disorders show relatively high levels of perfectionism—particularly self-oriented perfectionism—where the individuals have high standards for themselves but not for others. Two separate studies have confirmed that women with either AN or BN have equally high levels of perfectionism.

Individuals who struggle with AN tend to have high levels of harm avoidance. An individual who is harm avoidant is often worrisome, pessimistic, and shy in addition to lacking impulsivity or seeking novel things—also expressed as (showing signs of) novelty seeking. The binge/purge subtype of AN is often slightly higher in impulsivity and novelty seeking while the restricting subtype is higher in persistence. Researchers have linked higher levels of harm avoidance with higher levels of serotonin in the brain, and scientists have linked harm avoidance with specific alterations in the serotonin system in women recovered from AN.

A study measuring slightly different facets of personality found that women with either the restricting or binge/purge subtype of AN had higher levels of neuroticism characterized by depression, anxiety, worry, and moodiness than of controls, and that women with restricting AN scored higher on measures of agreeableness and conscientiousness than those with the binge/purge type.

Similar to individuals with AN, individuals with BN have high levels of harm avoidance, but it is often paired with high levels of novelty seeking.

Interestingly, a recent study found that individuals with the binge/purge subtype of AN show personality traits that look like a combination of restricting AN and BN. Other research has found high levels of anxiety, emotional dysregulation, and impulsivity in women with BN, and greater impulsivity was associated with more frequent compensatory behaviors. Researchers are also finding that individuals who struggle with regulating the amount of dopamine in their brains have higher levels of novelty seeking and that this also occurs in women with BN.

There is not as much research about personality traits of individuals with BED. Preliminary research around individuals with BED has found higher levels of harm avoidance and novelty seeking and lower levels of self-directedness than in individuals without BED. Individuals with BED also tend to have lower self-esteem and a greater sense of a lack of control in their life as well as feelings of inadequacy.

While there is a growing body of research around personality traits in individuals with eating disorders, it is also important to highlight that sustained starvation can prompt changes in interpersonal characteristics as well as cognition and behavior. For this reason, it can be difficult to discern the psychological causes for an eating disorder from the psychological effects of an eating disorder. For example, the comorbidity of depression and anxiety with eating disorders has raised the question as to whether these mental health disorders precede an eating disorder or are a result of an eating disorder.

Societal View of Body Image/Social Media

Evidence shows the societal view of body image as well as social media play a significant role in the development of eating disorders. Today, the most prevalent images in our society equate beauty with thinness for women and a lean, muscular build for men. Individuals who adhere to these beauty ideals have an increased risk of body dissatisfaction, which is known to lead to ED behaviors. It is also safe to say that those without eating disorders might also be impacted by the constant bombardment of unrealistic beauty ideals. An increase in access to global media and technological advances such as photoshop and airbrushing have further skewed our perception of attainable beauty standards.

In 1998, a research study was completed in rural Fiji as Western television was introduced to the area for the first time. Researchers found that the Fijians' exposure to Western television resulted in negative body image, compensatory behaviors to attempt to control weight, and a significant preoccupation with share and weight. The research study highlighted people's vulnerability to images supplied by the media. The research study also suggested that most individuals exposed to media do not necessarily develop clinically diagnosable eating disorders but individuals who already have risk factors might have increased vulnerability to media messages about weight and beauty and might even seek out exposure to them.

Trauma

Traumatic events such as abuse or neglect can often precede the development of an eating disorder. Guilt and shame as well as body dissatisfaction and feeling a lack of control over the body are often felt after a traumatic event. An eating disorder can presumably assuage guilt and shame or can serve as an attempt to regain control after trauma. In some cases, an eating disorder is an expression of self-harm or misdirected self-punishment for trauma. Anecdotally, one-half to two-thirds of individuals with eating disorders have experienced trauma.

Recent research highlights the importance of evaluating for trauma and post-traumatic stress disorder (PTSD) when treating eating disorders. A relationship between eating disorders, particularly BN and BED, and trauma has been discovered among participants in various research studies. While childhood sexual abuse has been identified as a risk factor for eating disorders, research is starting to suggest that trauma can also lead to the development of eating disorders. A recent research study described most individuals with eating disorders as having reported a history of interpersonal trauma. According to this research, approximately one-third of women with BN, one-fifth of women with BED, and one-tenth of women with other eating disorders met criteria for PTSD. Overall, the most significant finding in this research study was that rates of eating disorders were generally higher in people who experienced trauma and PTSD.

A study from 2007 shows that there are many types of trauma that can be associated with eating disorders, including teasing, bullying, neglect, emotional and physical neglect (including food deprivation), emotional abuse, sexual harassment, sexual assault, physical abuse, and assault. Furthermore, women who reported sexually related trauma were significantly more likely to exhibit psychopathology than controls, including higher rates of both diagnoses for eating disorders and PTSD.

It is uncertain exactly why trauma contributes to the development of an eating disorder, but it has recently been determined that trauma can create disruptions in the nervous system and disruptions in the nervous system can lead to an inability to manage emotions. As has been discussed, ED behaviors are often an effective avenue to manage emotions. Sexual trauma can also cause body image issues that are partly related to the self-deprecating view that can develop after sexual trauma. For example, some victims hope to become too thin or too heavy in order to reduce their attractiveness.

For an individual diagnosed with PTSD who has experienced sexual assault, the prevalence of BN is significantly greater in comparison to an individual without PTSD who has experienced sexual assault and to an individual who has no history of sexual assault. Summarily, these results suggest that it is PTSD rather than a history of sexual assault that best forecasts the emergence of BN.

When examined in greater detail, PTSD and eating disorders have several shared characteristics. Dissociation is common with both PTSD and eating disorders. ED behaviors are often an opportunity to effectively develop distance from disturbing thoughts, emotions, or memories associated with PTSD. Vomiting can be seen as a way to get rid of something unwanted (e.g., emotion or memory) while bingeing can be seen as a way to fill a void. Rationally, an individual knows that vomiting does not get rid of an unwanted thought or feeling. In addition, a void cannot be filled with food. Yet both provide relief for the individual either in managing the symptoms of PTSD or as a coping mechanism in dealing with an unresolved and possibly subconscious trauma.

Along with the shared characteristics between PTSD and eating disorders, there are also genetic and biological factors that might explain the correlation. However, even while there may be additional factors for this relationship between eating disorders and PTSD, studies continue to show that individuals with trauma as well as PTSD have a higher prevalence of eating disorders than the general population does. This suggests that, at the very least, eating disorders are much more complicated to treat than originally believed. This added layer of complexity must be understood in order to treat eating disorders, trauma, and PTSD effectively.

CAUSES AND RISK FACTORS THAT SPECIFICALLY AFFECT MINORITY GROUPS

Even today, the stereotype of an individual with an eating disorder is that of a young, educated, wealthy white woman, but eating disorders affect various genders, races, ethnicities, and sexual orientations—as well as some special groups, such as athletes—more than we think.

Men with Eating Disorders

Despite the stereotype that eating disorders are reserved for women, approximately one in three individuals struggling with an eating disorder is a man. In addition, disordered eating behaviors, including fasting, binge eating, purging, and laxative abuse, are nearly as common among men as they are among women. Unsurprisingly, men are far less likely to ask for help for his eating disorder. Fortunately, once a man finds help, his recovery rate becomes comparable to a woman's.

Several factors lead to men and boys being under- and undiagnosed for an eating disorder. For example, men and boys can face twice as much stigma for an eating disorder since it could be perceived as feminine or gay to have an eating disorder and it could be seen as weak to seek psychological help. Additionally, assessment batteries with language geared to women and girls have led to misconceptions about the nature of disordered eating in men.

There are numerous studies on men's body image, and results vary widely. Due to the media messages they are exposed to regularly, many men presumably feel that it is important to be muscular. Exposure to the unattainable images portrayed in the media are leading to more body dissatisfaction for men. The desire for increased musculature is not uncommon, and it crosses age groups. One-quarter of normal-weight men perceive themselves to be underweight, and almost 90 percent of teenage boys have suggested that they exercise with the goal of bulking up. Muscle dysmorphia, a subtype of body dysmorphic disorder, is an emerging disorder that primarily affects male body builders. Individuals with muscle dysmorphia obsess about being muscular, and their compulsions can include abnormal eating patterns, spending countless hours in the gym, spending excessive amounts of money on supplements, and even using steroids to achieve musculature.

Racial and Ethnic Minorities with Eating Disorders

Many studies have suggested that it is the westernization of non-Western cultures and of ethnic minorities living within Western cultures that is causing an increase in the incidence of eating disorders among individuals who are not white, that is, non-Caucasian. In other words, an individual who has been living in a non-Western culture that did not value thinness might become more susceptible to an eating disorder due to the intrusion of Western values related to thinness. Within the United States, for example, it is becoming evident that the risk for eating disorders is directly correlated to the level of acculturation or the degree to which a person adopts the values, attitudes, and identity of the dominant culture. This theory has recently been challenged by researchers who cite examples such as that of Curaçao, where, though it is culturally acceptable to be overweight, the prevalence of AN is as high as in Western nations. Similarly, a recent study showed few differences in the incidence of disordered eating between Iranian women living in the United States and those living in Iran, a country where Western media are banned. This study even considered the variable that the women living in Iran wore a full body covering that obscured size and shape. The results specifically showed that Iranian women living in Iran were more likely than Iranian women living in the United States to exercise excessively to lose weight, and to desire an empty stomach.

Continuing to better understand cultural differences may also be helpful in identifying more effective approaches for assessing and screening for eating disorders in various ethnicities and minorities. The key groups that have been studied most are women who identify as Latina, African American, or Asian American.

Latina Women

According to the research, Latina women are average in terms of self-esteem, specifically with regard to their weight and body satisfaction. Studies have shown that Latinas have body image concerns and eating disorders at rates comparable to or greater than non-Latina white women. Other research has demonstrated that Latina women in the United States struggle significantly with conflicting cultural expectations. While the white or Caucasian culture values a thinner body ideal, a larger body is generally more accepted in the Latinx culture. In addition, Latina women specifically might face more obstacles when seeking treatment for an eating disorder, due to the stigma of seeking psychological help in the Latinx culture and the high cost of appropriate treatment.

African American Women

According to the research, African American women generally have the highest self-esteem in general, the highest self-esteem regarding their weight, the greatest body satisfaction—regardless of their actual size—and the highest self-rating on sexual attractiveness when compared to women of other races. African American women are also the least likely to actively work to control their weight. It is hypothesized that the concept of beauty is more flexible in African American control, so self-esteem and body satisfaction can be higher. This attitude itself may be healthy, but rates of obesity are also higher in this group of women. Interestingly, Caucasians, Latinas, and African Americans differ significantly in their levels of body dissatisfaction and disordered eating behaviors, but they did not differ in their reports of binge eating.

Asian American Women

According to the research, Asian Americans appear to have explicit risks for eating disorders—specifically, a high incidence of AN. In one research study, wealthier, more achievement-oriented Asian women had greater concern about meeting parental expectations. Presumably, this could be correlated with perfectionism, a principal predictor of AN. Interestingly, fear of being fat or gaining weight is commonly absent in Asian Americans women with AN. This is notable because Asian Americans with eating disorders who complete standard ED questionnaires often appear to be less disordered than their non-Asian peers. Culturally, Asians and Asian Americans often deny or minimize symptoms of illnesses—including mental illnesses, especially since mental illnesses are considered taboo in the Asian culture. This could explain the absence of the fear of fatness in an eating disorder; however, AN without any self-reported fear of fatness exists in Western culture too.

Sexual Minorities with Eating Disorders

Individuals who identify as lesbian, gay, or bisexual (LGB) experience unique stressors that may contribute to the development of an eating disorder. While there is still much research to be done on the relationships between sexuality, gender identity, body image, and eating disorders, we know that eating disorders disproportionately impact some segments of the LGB community. Research shows that, beginning as early as 12 years of age, LGB teens may be at higher risk for binge eating and purging behaviors than their heterosexual peers are. According to the National Eating Disorders Association (NEDA), potential factors that may play a role in the development of an eating disorder may include negative self-talk, fear of rejection or actual rejection, discrimination, bullying, experiences of violence and PTSD due to sexual orientation and/or gender identity, in addition to discordance between gender assigned at birth and gender expression, and inability to meet body image ideals within some LGBTQ+ cultural contexts.

According to NEDA, LGBTQ+ individuals, in addition to experiencing unique contributing factors for eating disorders, may also face challenges for accessing treatment and support. Common obstacles might include the lack of culturally competent treatment providers to address the complexity of unique sexuality and gender identity issues, insufficient eating disorders education among LGBTQ+ resource providers who are in a position to assess and intervene, and lack of support from family and friends.

While the research remains limited on eating disorders among LGBTQ+ populations, NEDA has secured some statistics on eating disorders in connection with individuals who identify as LGBTQ+. Boys who identify as gay or bisexual are more likely to have engaged in ED behaviors than boys who identify as heterosexual, and men who identify as gay or bisexual have a significantly higher prevalence of subclinical eating disorders as well as BN than men who identify as heterosexual. Men who identify as gay are seven times more likely to report bingeing and 12 times more likely to report purging than men who identify as heterosexual do. And while gay men represent only 5 percent of the total population, approximately 42 percent of men who have an eating disorder identify as gay. Women identifying as lesbian, bisexual, or mostly heterosexual were twice as likely to report binge eating, and there is an elevated prevalence of binge eating as well as compensatory behaviors for all people who identified as gay, lesbian, bisexual, or mostly heterosexual in comparison to their heterosexual peers. Finally, there is a presumably protective factor if an LGBTQ+ individual feels connected to the LGBTQ+ community, because fewer episodes of eating disorders are reported in such cases.

Athletes with Eating Disorders

There is a lot of mixed information about athletes and eating disorders. One study found the number of college athletes at risk for developing AN or BN to be 35 percent or 58 percent for women and 10 percent or 38 percent for men. respectively. Another study suggested that 1 percent of all college student athletes have an eating disorder. There are risk factors as well as protective factors for athletes involved in sport; these will be explored further.

Protective Factors for Eating Disorders. There are a number of factors that can be considered protective factors for eating disorders for athletes. For example, coaches who emphasize factors that contribute to personal success, such as motivation and enthusiasm rather than body weight or shape, and display a positive, person-oriented coaching style rather than a negative, performance-oriented coaching style are protective factors for athletes. Coaches and parents who educate, talk about, and support the changing female body are also protective factors. The same is true for social influence and support from teammates with healthy attitudes toward size and shape.

Risk Factors for Eating Disorders. Athletics are a great way to build self-esteem, promote physical health and exercise, and demonstrate the value of teamwork, but not all athletic stressors are constructive. The pressure to succeed and an emphasis on body weight and shape can create a tough environment for athletes to thrive in. Unfortunately, athletic competition can be a factor contributing to psychological and physical stress. When the pressures of athletic competition are added to an existing cultural emphasis on thinness, the risks increase for athletes to develop disordered eating, according to *Mind, Body and Sport,* a handbook published by the National Collegiate Athletic Association (NCAA).

Mind, Body and Sport also notes that emphasis on reducing body weight or body fat to enhance sport performance can result in weight pressures on the athlete from coaches or even teammates, which increases the risk of restrictive dieting as well as the use of weight loss methods and disordered eating. Even individual athletes' perception that their coaches think they need to lose weight can heighten weight pressures and increase the risk of disordered eating.

Coaches have considerable influence on their athletes, and it appears that their relationship with their athletes—and more specifically their motivational climate—can influence the risk of disordered eating. A relationship between coach and athlete characterized by high conflict and low support has been associated with increased disordered eating among athletes. Additionally, an ego/performance-centered motivational climate as opposed to a skills-mastery climate has been associated with an increased risk of disordered eating.

For some athletes, revealing uniforms can increase body consciousness, body dissatisfaction, and the use of compensatory methods to lose weight. One study suggested that almost half of swimmers surveyed considered their swimsuit to be a stressor. Another research study explained that volleyball players often experience decreased self-esteem related to their body and also found the revealing uniforms to be distracting and to negatively impact their sport performance.

The relationship between body image and body dissatisfaction in athletes who are women is more complicated than in the general population. Women in sports actually have two body images—one within sport and one outside of sport—and disordered eating or an eating disorder can occur in either context or both. For example, a woman in sport might appreciate that her muscular body facilitates sport performance but feel conflicted about her body type when dating, because she might feel she does not meet societal norms of femininity.

There are also sports or categories of sports that are more likely to include athletes with eating disorders. Sports that emphasize appearance, weight requirements, or muscularity such as gymnastics, diving, bodybuilding, and wrestling have a higher prevalence rate of eating disorders. According to one study, more than 70 percent of elite athletes in weight-class sports diet and experience abnormal eating behaviors. Sports that focus on the individual rather than the entire team, such as gymnastics, running, figure skating, dance, or diving, also have a higher prevalence of eating disorders.

Difficulty with Diagnosis of Eating Disorders in Sport. Another risk to athletes relates to aspects of the sport environment that make identification of eating disorders more difficult. In sport, athletes are often expected to have a particular body shape or size dependent on the sport (e.g., thinness for a distance runner). Such stereotypes in sport can affect the perception of coaches and spectators as well as family and friends; because the athletes fit the stereotype, they are less likely to be identified as having a problem related to eating. Identification is also influenced by performance, and athletes are also less likely to be identified if their performance in sport is good.

In addition, ED symptoms such as controlling weight and hour of training may be misperceived as normal or even desirable in the sport environment. Personality characteristics and behaviors comparable to individuals diagnosed with eating (e.g., perfectionism and excessive training) may be misperceived as good athlete traits.

Clearly, there are a number of contributions to the development of an eating disorder as well as varying prevalence rates based on gender, race or ethnicity, sexual orientation, and other group membership. In the next chapter, we will look into the signs and symptoms of an eating disorder.

4

Signs and Symptoms

While many assume that an eating disorder is identifiable from an initial physical impression, such as low weight, there are many other ways to spot the start or progression of this illness. Not only can physical attributes send a signal that something may not be right but also the ways in which individuals interact with others, present emotionally, process information, and/or alter their lifestyle in certain ways can hint that something may be of concern and in need of more attention. Identifying an eating disorder can also come with obstacles that often lengthen one's struggle and, unfortunately, lead to more severe consequences. This chapter is intended to help recognize an eating disorder in yourself or others, as well as shed light on barriers that can prevent distinguishing concern. This chapter will also include some of the signs that someone is engaging in disordered eating and moving in a direction toward an eating disorder.

As you read, it is important to be aware that there is a general distinction between signs and symptoms, even though there can be overlap as well. Signs can be observed by another person, such as a doctor or family member, while symptoms are felt or noticed internally by the individual.

PHYSICAL SIGNS

Of Anorexia Nervosa

Even though anorexia is one of the more noticeable types of eating disorders due to some obvious physical signs, there are also many red flags that go unnoticed and are not as visible to the eye. A person who is struggling with anorexia often endures dramatic weight loss due to restriction, overexercise, and/or compensatory behaviors. The decrease in weight can be a gradual trend or sometimes much more rapid, depending on the severity of the behaviors. Maintaining a healthy, appropriate weight becomes more challenging the deeper one gets into the eating disorder. Those suffering from anorexia are often seen dressing in layers due to colder body temperatures. Cold hands and feet are common because of inadequate nutrition, low body fat, and the body's difficulty regulating temperature and conserving energy. Fat helps us tolerate colder temperatures, so when one's rigidity around food includes restriction of high-fat or high-calories food, this often results in the need for extra clothing layers, even in mild temperatures.

Dry skin and brittle nails occur when there is a depletion of calories, protein, and other essential minerals and vitamins. Thin hair on the body, commonly called lanugo, is another usual physical sign observable in those with anorexia exclusively. When the body senses a decrease in fat storage, it responds by creating extra hair to provide warmth, often on the face, back, arms, and chest. This is another way the body tries to protect itself when in distress. The skin itself can also suffer damage as a result of malnutrition. Bruising, tearing, and popped blood vessels are only a few examples of evident changes. Skin may also appear more crinkled with less muscle and fat.

Those with anorexia frequently feel dizzy and exhausted, as well as experience muscle weakness. This can escalate to the point of passing out or fainting, which happens when the brain is not getting enough blood. Dehydration, low blood sugar, and irregular blood pressure triggered by insufficient nutritional intake are also contributors to overall weakness and fatigue. Anemia, which causes weakness and tiredness, results from not obtaining enough iron, which we get from iron-rich foods such as meat, beans, nuts, and seeds. These types of food not only help your body better absorb iron but also increase red blood cell count to guarantee oxygen-rich blood is circulating within your body. Additionally, a weakened immune system caused by anemia and a low white blood count make it difficult to rebound from sickness. These physical setbacks also influence and inhibit basic healing properties, like a cut needing to close up.

When the body does not receive the needed amounts of fat and cholesterol through food, and/or if the food is compensated for by exercise or purging, hormone levels can become out of whack. When a hormone such as GnRH, which instigates a menstrual cycle, is slow to produce or not producing at all, it can cause irregular menstrual cycles or a complete loss of a menstrual cycle, also known as amenorrhea. Amenorrhea was previously one of the requisites for anorexia nervosa (AN) in the *DSM*-IV. The issue with this was that amenorrhea not only eliminated males from obtaining an appropriate diagnosis but also eliminated females who continued to have a period despite showing other symptoms qualifying them for the diagnosis of anorexia.

A more recent explanation of what causes the body to stop a cycle due to low weight was produced by Mountjoy and colleagues in 2015, specifically with the intention of protecting athletes: when there is an imbalance between one's energy intake, or their amount of food, and the energy they are expending, most often through exercise, there are many physical, psychological, physiological, and health-related consequences. This can be especially concerning for athletes, which we will go into more detail about in a later chapter.

Of Bulimia Nervosa

Physically identifying someone with bulimia by weight or physical appearance is different than with anorexia because most people struggling with bulimia are of normal or above normal weight. Repetitive vomiting has a multitude of physical effects on the body. One common visible sign of bulimia is swollen salivary glands that cause swelling in the cheeks or jawline. Purging is also observable by cuts on one's fingers and/or hands. Cavities, sensitive and discolored teeth, and the erosion of tooth enamel from the acid produced by recurrent vomiting also occur in those struggling with bulimic behaviors. Purging can cause significant dehydration, which is visible through lab work, but also physical symptoms such as increased thirst, muscle cramps, dry mouth, and lightheadedness.

While there can be an assumption that purging refers solely to self-induced vomiting, there are many other forms of purging common in both bulimia and anorexia that have severe consequences. Overexercise, which is typically used to rid oneself of unwanted calories, can be visible in severe musculoskeletal damage, stress fractures, broken bones, and general pain. If you have bones that are weak for your age and prone to fractures, it may be a sign that you have osteopenia or osteoporosis, which can be a long-term complication of an eating disorder. This will be further explained in chapter 6.

The use of laxatives, diuretics, and enemas, which are all intended to relieve constipation by rushing food content through one's body faster than the human body is designed to do so, is another sign one is struggling with an eating disorder. The use can either be well hidden or more obvious, depending on frequency of use and the secrecy employed. In addition to lethal effects, irritable bowel syndrome and bowel tumors can be indications one is misusing laxatives, diuretics, and enemas. These behaviors can also show up in electrolyte and other essential mineral deficiencies, which all require medical care and frequent hospitalizations. Additionally, one may experience muscle cramps, spasms, abnormal heart rhythms, and, in worst-case scenarios, cessation of a heartbeat with the use of laxatives or enemas.

The use of supplements and vitamins advertised to help with weight loss is a common sign of all types of eating disorders. Despite the harmful side effects, the demand for these products is only increasing, which makes their use a more common practice within ED behaviors. The Food and Drug Administration (FDA) has banned many ingredients used to make the supplements that are advertised to burn fat or speed up metabolism. Often these products are not approved or regulated in the United States and contain unsafe and toxic ingredients not included on the labels. It is important to note that some FDA-approved supplements still make it to the shelves, despite their damaging effects.

The use of street drugs, specifically stimulants and amphetamines, to lose weight may be another indicator that someone has an eating disorder. These drugs are intended to suppress the appetite, but, as with many compensatory behaviors utilized when struggling with an eating disorder, there are serious risks, including drug addiction, psychological issues, and dangerous physical effects.

Of Binge Eating Disorder

Frequent interest in various diets, as well as an instability of weight due to large amounts of food intake, are common physical signs of binge eating disorder. This often results in feeling uncomfortably full and out of control once one starts to eat. One will often be observed eating binge-type foods and amounts, which can vary from person to person, at a fast pace. Some of the recurrently observed medical symptoms resulting from these behaviors include gastrointestinal problems, abnormal blood pressure levels, and high cholesterol, as well as a predisposition to type 2 diabetes, which happens when the body is unable to use insulin appropriately. Those at a higher weight, which can be induced by binge eating, are also at risk for developing sleep apnea. This condition presents as irregular breathing patterns while sleeping, specifically when one stops breathing for 10 seconds or more during sleep.

Commonalities among All Types of Eating Disorders

While we have reviewed some of the noticeable signs and symptoms specific to each of the more common eating disorders and behavior patterns, there are also physical indicators shared among all types of eating disorders. One sign we see across the board is the strong attraction or fixation toward fad diets. Fad diets are more trendy recommendations for weight loss or other health benefits; they make false promises that are most often unrealistic. Examples include the paleo, low-carb, and ketogenic diets. Often, they are sponsored or endorsed by celebrities or those in the public eye.

Another shared physical marker that is crucial when identifying an eating disorder is abnormality of labs. Potassium, sodium, glucose, phosphorus, magnesium, and blood counts that are not within normal ranges are just a few examples of the more common indicators of concern. These can help identify nutritional deficiencies, electrolyte imbalances, anemia, hormone discrepancies, and dehydration caused by behavior such as purging or laxative use. Fluid changes within the body can occur when there are unhealthy compensatory behaviors, described above, or inadequate intake, as well as indigestion and constipation. When these changes happen, it is not unheard of for one's feet and hands to swell. Muscle weakness and general fatigue are also very common when the body is not appropriately nourished, which can occur from all types of ED behaviors.

Not only can actual ED behaviors interfere with getting enough sleep, especially if they tend to happen later in the night, but the physical effects of eating disorders described throughout this section can also lead to inconsistent and unhealthy sleep patterns. This is because the body's efforts to regulate and function normally are being disrupted. Some people suffer from an actual sleep-related eating disorder. This occurs when a person is unaware of waking and eating—often large amounts of food—during the night. The presence of another person who can witness and report on such behaviors can be helpful when someone is suspected of being in need of help.

EMOTIONAL SIGNS

Someone who is struggling with an eating disorder will also regularly display emotional signs that could signal distress. These signs are often difficult to identify due to previous efforts masking, numbing, or avoiding any connection with feelings by using ED behaviors. While eating disorders can involve preoccupation with physical appearance and can seem obvious to an outside observer, there are many unseen and invisible emotional factors that can generate red flags and help identify concern. Knowing what these may look like is important for helping not only oneself but also close friends or family members.

Those denying a need for food and consequently rejecting opportunities or offered support to eat, are possibly struggling with an eating disorder, most likely AN. Comments about being or feeling "fat," even though "fat" is not truly a feeling, signify an intense fear of gaining weight and dissatisfaction with one's body weight or size. This fear extends to any actual changes or perceived flaws relative to one's body, which intensifies an inaccurate and negative self-image. As a result of this preoccupation and alarm, experiencing guilt, disgust, and shame about what one eats, as well as making efforts to get rid of or compensate for food, is common. These feelings are not exclusive to those engaging in binge eating episodes, as they can result from any amount of food or behavior. As previously described, excessive worry about physical appearance, body weight, shape, and size is a telltale sign of an eating disorder but can also lead to immediate mood swings. Seeing a reflection in a mirror and a number on the scale are both examples of precursors to a shift in how you feel about yourself; as well as your perception of how others view you.

Depressive feelings, such as a lack of interest in activities one used to enjoy, irritability, withdrawal from friends, loneliness, and anxiety, are all reflections of possible changes in one's mood that are commonly experienced alongside an eating disorder. Low self-esteem, which may also look like uncertainty of oneself or a decrease in self-confidence or worth, is another common indicator of emotional distress that can accompany an eating disorder. An additional emotional sign observed externally is unease or worry when plans are disrupted or change unexpectedly. Many of these emotional experiences often continue while someone is in treatment. This is because behaviors previously used to cope with uncomfortable emotions are taken away, and the person is then forced to connect with the emotions more directly rather than push them away.

Comorbidity, which refers to the occurrence of two disorders at the same time, is very common with an ED presentation. A few examples of commonly occurring disorders during the presence of an eating disorder include, but are not limited to, mood disorders, post-traumatic stress disorder, and obsessive-compulsive disorder. The chicken or egg conundrum is relevant to eating disorders and emotions. This is because some feelings serve as precursors for the development of an eating disorder, while other emotional symptoms come after an eating disorder has developed. This scenario is not always easy to puzzle out and requires time to explore.

Something important to note is that when individuals who hide their emotional struggles often, in the same way, conceal their actual ED behaviors, they are likely working to keep the spotlight off themselves.

Minimizing or denying another person's observation of a mood change or shift in temperament may be a warning that the one struggling is working hard to keep the attention away from the struggle or distress.

COGNITIVE SIGNS

Eating disorders can have a profound impact on individuals' mental capacity and how they think. When the body is being starved, the brain, which is one of the bodily organs, is also suffering because it is no longer getting adequate nutrition to perform its routine tasks. In the same way a body becomes fatigued and void of energy, the brain's functioning is also compromised as a result of ED behaviors. These can have an effect on brain chemicals, which consequently affect aspects such as learning and motivation levels. We will go into much more detail in chapter 6 when discussing some of the current research highlighting specific changes within the brain that result from ED behaviors, as well as how brain imaging may give us insight into the predisposition of the development of an eating disorder.

A shortage or inconsistency of necessary food intake may lead to difficulty with memory, concentration, decision-making, and judgment. Someone searching for words or repeatedly feeling frustrated losing a thought is also a sign that cognition could be impacted. This impact is often not only frustrating for individuals with eating disorders but also noticeable for others around them. A recognizable shift occurs that is often not corrected until the person comes back "online." Some describe this moment as flipping a light switch, because the differences in how they feel when fueling their body appropriately versus when they were struggling become more obvious.

Rigid preoccupation or fixation around specifics of food is another noticeable sign of an eating disorder. Someone regularly counting calories, macros, or fat grams, as well as someone hoarding for binge purposes, will struggle to take a break from this practice. You might imagine this cycle as reflective of tunnel vision, where no other option exists any longer and the eating disorder further exerts more control over the person's life. Often it becomes a central, often obsessive, part of daily routine that cannot be disrupted. Intellectually working to separate from this pattern becomes overwhelming and feels impossible without a greater level of support and intervention.

Lastly, a commonality among thought processes of many people with an eating disorder is their inaccurate perception of their body weight, shape, or size. Even the earlier researchers in this field, such as Hilde Bruch, initiated a link between one's behaviors and body image, which is often negative and distorted. The desire to further look at ways self-acceptance is influenced by individuals' perception of their physical body image continues to grow. We know we are never truly able to attain an exact perception of our body—only a reflection from a mirror or description from someone else—but many become fused, or attached, to what they *think* they see through their own eyes. When people use harmful behaviors to try changing or controlling their appearance, it can have long-lasting effects on the progression of an eating disorder. Among those who are significantly underweight, there is also a persistent inability to recognize concerns or consequences resulting from their declining weight or increasing behaviors. Similarly, those who may be risking medical complications, such as heart issues or diabetes, because their weight is exceeding a normal, healthy range may be using weight as a protection or mask from something. It can make it hard for them to hear expressed concerns and take them seriously enough to accept help. An observer of someone who is struggling, one who points out noticeable differences and expresses worries, is often met with resistance, denial, and at times, further isolation. This is because the eating disorder and its related routines can serve as an outlet for control. When those become threatened, individuals with eating disorders will work to protect what they fear losing most. This is especially difficult when they are cognitively unable to gain a realistic picture of the harm they are facing.

INTERPERSONAL SIGNS

Relationally, there are noticeable signs or red flags that occur among those whom persons with eating disorders are around most often, such as friends, family, classmates, teammates, or individuals from their work setting. Interactions may start to change, and an intuitive impression that things are shifting on an interpersonal level between you and someone else could signal the need to help this person seek support. It is important to take these cues seriously.

Some examples of these social interactions or shifts would include increased fear and discomfort with regard to eating in front of others. Frequently, social events such as dinners, birthday parties, or holiday festivities are avoided with the intention of isolating oneself, especially when food is involved. Avoiding embarrassment around particular eating patterns is another reason for the withdrawal. Individuals would rather not be in a situation where they would have to mask their ED behaviors or unwillingness to eat with everyone else. Instead, they may choose to avoid the occasion altogether and will eventually start to provide reasons or excuses for disappearing regularly from specific events, gatherings, and social

get-togethers. This begins to limit contact with others and decreases the amount of time spent connecting with others interpersonally. For example, athletes who are having a difficult time with adequate food intake or over-exercise may begin missing team dinners, spending more time at the gym, or intentionally planning other obligations during team events that involve food. Another example would be a student who begins studying more often during the lunch period and consequently avoids eating in the cafeteria with peers.

It may come as a surprise, but those who are struggling with an eating disorder often actually enjoy cooking for others but not eating the food they themselves prepared. This is typically a way to distract from their avoidance of the food, keep the attention on something else, and mask their fear of actually having to eat in front of others. There is also an element of people-pleasing that is quite pervasive in the temperaments of those struggling with eating disorders, specifically those diagnosed with anorexia, restricting type. Methods of caretaking, such as preparing meals, are very common.

Making sudden plans or joining a social gathering at the last minute is not something persons who are struggling with an eating disorder would be prone to do. In the same way ED behaviors provide some form of control, routine, and structure, making plans ahead of time and knowing exactly how these plans will unfold is ideal in their mind. When a plan shifts or the option for joining a social engagement last minute comes about, it is often met with resistance and, often, the decision not to partake. Spending time alone in the illness becomes more of a preference.

Finally, eating disorders truly thrive on secrecy and manipulation. Tactics and behaviors that function to keep them hidden and mask what is actually occurring often start to become more visible within relationships and interactions. Efforts to hide themselves and their habits will become more noticeable in individuals' normal routine, whether in a work, family, or school situation.

BEHAVIORAL CHANGES IN LIFESTYLE

There are many similarities between recognizing the interpersonal signals of an eating disorder and observing the shifts within an affected person's behavior or daily routine. Both can be helpful ways of identifying someone in need of support. Intentional withdrawal from one's typical social routine or community circle may be a clear indicator of deliberate isolation as well as another way for the eating disorder to gain or maintain control. Often this void of interaction with others becomes filled with other tasks, to-do lists, or just time spent alone and out of the public or social eye. A profound sense of rigidity and inflexibility within one's life-style begins to sway an individual away from opportunities to join in on plans last minute, and overall contact with others decreases.

There is often an intentional avoidance of scheduling meals with others or partaking in events involving food. This is not only within a social set-ting but also on an individual level. Changes within one's food intake and variety, whether increases or decreases, can be visible as well. They may also reflect variation in the number of times one goes grocery shopping or orders food, depending on the role food plays in one's eating disorder. For someone struggling with the anorexia, restricting type, grocery stores and restaurants are often highly avoided, while someone engaging in binge eat-ing behaviors may be frequenting stores more often. For those struggling with orthorexic tendencies, there may be a fixation on only purchasing from health food stores due to what they perceive and strongly believe to be healthy foods devoid of artificial ingredients, genetic changes, and so on. Food options become narrowed, and many products are eliminated completely.

Interpersonally, relationships regularly suffer because of the secrecy, efforts to maintain control, and isolation that occur when someone has an eating disorder. Often a partner, friend, or family member is left feeling lost and helpless while the individual with the illness continues to pull fur-ther away. On a more intimate level, a decrease in sex is often a reflection of self-consciousness and negative body image thoughts as well as protec-tion from past distress or trauma.

While eating disorders are themselves a type a self-harm, additional forms of hurting oneself and suicidality are commonly observed within someone who is struggling. Recognition of physical markers of self-harm, such as cutting or burning, as well as comments indicating a wish to die or a "what's the point?" attitude would all be strong causes for seeking sup-port for someone immediately. This becomes more challenging the harder individuals work to avoid being around others and hide the level of pain they are experiencing.

A more obvious and external indicator in their lifestyle is the attempt they make to consistently get rid of food or calories. Examples include exercise or supplements that promote self-induced purging through use of laxatives, diuretics, or vomiting. Again, they will commonly try to hide these behaviors. However, when the ED voice is extremely loud, keeping the behaviors a secret can become less of a priority and, instead, more obvious to those who are around the struggling person on a consistent basis.

Bizarre food combinations as well as specific eating rituals or behaviors are also evidence of an eating disorder. Counting, ordering, picking at, moving food around on a plate, avoiding, and inconsistent pace are all

examples of mealtime behaviors that might be observed in someone struggling with eating the food as normally intended. These behaviors are ways
to distract and stall from doing what the person fears most and also to
manipulate the food and change it from its intended form or purpose,
which is called a control mechanism.

There are also behavioral or lifestyle changes specific to someone who
struggles with binge eating behaviors. These may include storing large
quantities of food or food containers as well as hoarding. Hoarding occurs
when people have trouble giving up or limiting a quantity of food in their
possession and is often done in secret due to embarrassment and shame.
Both large-scale storing and hoarding can also reflect an extreme amount of
money being spent on food, which can lead to financial stress. These quantities of food may also disappear faster than usual. Similar to those intentionally avoiding events or gatherings with food involved, schedules and plans
become focused around strategic or intended binge eating episodes.

Those using compensatory behaviors to get rid of the food consumed
may also be seen storing or acquiring large quantities of food. Additionally, there is often evidence of purging, despite the intended secrecy around
this pattern. Gum, water, hard candy, and the like are frequently used to
mask the smell or other signs of vomiting. Frequent bathroom use is also a
sign to be aware of.

Disordered Eating

Disordered eating refers to eating patterns or behaviors that resemble
symptoms of an eating disorder; however, altogether, the frequency, intensity, and severity are not enough to warrant the diagnosis of an eating disorder. However, disordered eating can be an antecedent to an eventual
eating disorder; it also is very challenging to identify, for a variety of reasons, and often goes unnoticed. First, social media and many aspects of
our society and culture perpetuate an intense focus around an ideal body
image, support fad diets, and encourage efforts to manipulate one's body
weight, shape, and size from a young age. In fact, a significantly higher
percentage of people struggle with disordered eating than those diagnosed
with a specific type of eating disorder. When disordered behaviors are
viewed as the norm, they become a template, and the motivation to interrupt the behaviors is not very high either for oneself or for others. Additionally, concern is less commonly expressed by others because the impact
of disordered eating on one's level of physical, emotional, and/or psychological functioning is not as severe as it could be with an eating disorder.

Disordered eating behaviors do not present obvious signs to others or
concerning symptoms to the individual, which thwarts alarm, continued

observation, and attempts to interrupt. For example, by definition, someone with anorexia must significantly restrict to the point of achieving a very low weight. On the contrary, someone could be engaging in anorexia-like behaviors or thoughts, such as calorie counting, excessive exercise, holding an intense fear around food, or restricting certain foods, but be of normal weight. One might also have a distorted view of one's but still be within a healthy weight range. The number of behavior episodes per week and the duration, or how long one has been using specific behaviors, also distinguish disordered eating patterns from an actual eating disorder.

It is important to evaluate the function or purpose behind the behaviors being used. Some areas of functioning to assess with regard to the possible impact of someone's disordered eating include, but are not limited to, interpersonal, social, professional, academic, cognitive areas, and self-care. Looking closely at how much certain behaviors interfere with one's ability to fully take part in each of these realms can help distinguish between disordered eating and an eating disorder.

BARRIERS TO IDENTIFYING AN EATING DISORDER

You may be faced with many obstacles to recognizing signs and symptoms of an eating disorder. As mentioned above, eating disorders flourish in secrecy, so the great lengths and efforts one makes to hide behaviors often mask red flags.

Paralleling one's attempts to conceal problematic patterns, one of the most concerning barriers is the lack of information that lab work can provide, especially in those struggling with anorexia, restricting type. Often, individuals are told by a medical professional that their labs look "good" or "within normal limits," thus disqualifying any concern or necessary referral to a specialist. This is typically because routine labs are assessing general stabilization, and specialty labs, which could pick up on more concerning consequences of behaviors, are not frequently ordered unless the illness has been identified.

Praise for "eating healthy" is also a way one hides severe restriction, avoidance of particular food groups, such as fats or starches, and rigid behaviors aimed at controlling weight. Being of normal weight or overweight can also be a visible barrier to identifying an eating disorder, especially with bulimic or binge-eating behaviors.

Isolation is also a significant indicator something may be wrong, but it keeps the issue hidden. The intention of spending more time alone is not only a means of avoidance but also a form of coping with uncomfortable or unfamiliar feelings. ED behaviors can serve to temporarily *manage* a wide range of emotions, but they also increase the time people spend in their illness and in working to hide behaviors. Isolation may also be the result of fearing judgment or critique from others. We know self-criticism is common within the individual, but escaping the chance that others will also provide evaluation or express worry is strongly preferred. Unfortunately, this withdrawal from others in general, and from work, school, or family settings in particular, can be even more detrimental to one's illness because of the loss of connection to support and structure, which makes the illness hard to identify.

One of the most common barriers is the inability to see beyond the belief that if the affected individuals would *just eat*, they would be cured. Eating disorders are not just about food. In fact, there is a reason that the biological-psychological-social model is one of the most common ways of conceptualizing and planning for treatment of an eating disorder. Past experiences, traumas, co-occurring disorders, and personality and temperament characteristics are only a few areas of contribution to the development and maintenance of an eating disorder. Many of these elements are not always visible to the eye or recognizable to those other than the person who is struggling. Often, even the individuals are unable to recognize the level of influence their eating disorder has over life and ability to function. Without being able to read minds, it is often hard to truly know what may be happening. Further, the multidimensional expression of an eating disorder is different for every person, regardless of the specific type or presentation. As described above, it can be challenging to parse out disordered eating behaviors, behaviors specific to a norm or culture— such as an athletic setting—orthorexic tendencies, and a full-blown eating disorder.

Myths and biases regarding who is more prone to developing or presenting with an eating disorder lead to frequent misperception for those who may in trouble. The idea that only women or those underweight can develop an eating disorder steers attention away from many others who have an equally great chance but may not look *sick enough* to be in danger.

As we will explore later on, there are some jobs, routines, or passions that involve particular practices that may resemble or align with particular ED behaviors. Sports and certain professions that have increased focus and pressure around appearance are both examples of potential areas that get overlooked due to the belief this is part of their norm or model. It never hurts to be curious and ask questions if hints warrant any level of concern.

As you can see, eating disorders and disordered eating behaviors can occur in anyone, despite how hard one works to mask concerning behaviors or how normal a particular pattern appears to fit within one's routine or community. The complex nature of this illness, coupled with the misperceptions regarding what an eating disorder looks like and who may struggle, make it difficult for observers, as well as the individuals them-selves, to pick up on. While treating clinicians utilize the *DSM* to identify, guide, and devise effective and individualized treatment approaches, knowledge and awareness of the changes this diagnostic tool has under-gone can provide even more insight into how an eating disorder may present—again, for family members and friends and those struggling themselves. This next chapter will explore the most recent revisions of the *DSM-5* as well as the most effective methods for assessing and treating an eating disorder in order to prevent further progression into a more severe state. Content regarding the comorbidity of eating disorders, as well as dif-ferential diagnoses, will also be covered.

5

Diagnosis, Treatment, and Management

There are a number of important considerations when diagnosing, treating, and managing eating disorders. Through the years, there have been many changes to how we diagnose eating disorders and even more changes to how we assess eating disorders. Fortunately, as more has been learned about how to diagnose and assess eating disorders, more treatment options have been developed and evaluated for efficacy.

CHANGES FROM *DSM*-IV-TR TO *DSM*-5

Before the fifth edition of the *Diagnostic and Statistical Manual of Mental Disorders* (*DSM*-5), the *Diagnostic and Statistical Manual of Mental Disorders*, fourth edition with text Revision or the *DSM*-IV-TR, had a chapter on eating disorders that included anorexia nervosa (AN) and bulimia nervosa (BN) in addition to eating disorder not otherwise specified (EDNOS). Other disorders, such as avoidant/restrictive food intake disorder (ARFID), pica, and rumination were discussed in the *DSM*-IV-TR, but they were included in a chapter called "Disorders Usually First Diagnosed in Infancy, Childhood, or Adolescence," which does not exist in the *DSM*-5. In the newest diagnostic and statistical manual, all the disorders previously mentioned in addition to some new disorders, including binge eating disorder (BED), have been added to a chapter called "Feeding and Eating Disorders." According to the *DSM*-5, feeding and eating disorders are defined as an ongoing disturbance of eating or eating-related behavior that can result in the altered absorption or consumption of food with a significant impairment in psychosocial functioning or physical health.

In addition to changes related to the location of some of the eating disorders, there were also changes made to some of the disorders themselves.

Pica, Rumination Disorder, and Avoidant Restrictive Food Intake Disorder

The criteria to diagnose pica and rumination disorder have not changed, but the location of these disorders changed from "Disorders Usually First Diagnosed in Infancy, Childhood, or Adolescence" in the DSM-IV-TR to "Feeding and Eating Disorders" in the DSM-5. In the DSM-IV-TR, the feeding disorder of infancy and early childhood was diagnosed when infants or children continued to fail at nourishing their body, resulting in an inability to gain or even maintain a healthy weight for more than a month. The primary problem was a disturbance in feeding or eating not related to an associated medical or gastrointestinal condition. The disorder also required an onset before the age of six. With the addition of ARFID to the DSM-5, those criteria remain the same, but there is a new criterion that suggests a significant nutritional deficiency and reliance on tube feeding or nutritional supplements. The diagnosis is also more specific in stating that the feeding or eating issues could be attributed to the sensory characteristics of food (e.g., taste or texture) or a concern about negative consequences of eating (e.g., nausea). Another new criterion also suggests that a lack of available food or an associated, culturally sanctioned practice (e.g., fasting for Ramadan) cannot account for the feeding or eating issues. The other criteria remain the same (e.g., ARFID cannot occur if AN or BN is a more appropriate diagnosis; the condition cannot be related to a medical condition).

Anorexia Nervosa

There are several significant changes in the criteria for diagnosing AN from DSM-IV-TR to DSM-5. The two greatest changes exist within the first criterion for an AN diagnosis. The first criterion previously included the language that individuals refused to maintain their body weight. This has been modified to suggest that there is a problem with the restriction of energy intake relative to requirements—for example, an individual is not eating enough food for what the body needs to function. Another change to the first criterion is recognizing that an individual has a significantly low weight in relation to the body, as opposed to being less than a specific body weight or below 85 percent of the expected weight. Historically, the second criterion for AN discussed a fear of becoming fat or gaining weight, but it has now added that persistent behaviors that interfere with gaining weight are also needed. The third criterion in the *DSM-5* is like that of the previous edition, but it has replaced denial of the risks of being underweight with persistent lack of recognition of risks posed by being underweight. The fourth criterion for AN, the cessation of menstruation, was removed altogether from the *DSM-5*. This criterion only applied to females who had begun to menstruate and inherently excluded all males as well as those females who had not reached puberty and females who had reached menopause.

As in the *DSM-IV-TR*, the criteria for AN in the *DSM-5* include specifiers of restricting, or binge eating/purging types. The language in the new edition is comparable to the earlier editions but is clearer, stating that the specifier applies to the previous three months as opposed to the more vaguely stated "current episode" (APA, *DSM-5*). Like other diagnoses in the *DSM-5*, the criteria for AN now include specifiers regarding severity and remission status. The severity specifier uses body mass index (BMI) with four levels of severity: extreme (BMI < 15 kg/m^2), severe (BMI = 15–15.99 kg/m^2), moderate (BMI = 16–16.99 kg/m^2) and mild (BMI ≥ 17 kg/m^2). These ranges are adapted from the World Health Organization categories for thinness in adults. For children and adolescents, clinicians are encouraged to use the BMI percentiles.

Bulimia Nervosa

The diagnosis of BN is fundamentally the same in the *DSM-5* as in earlier *DSM* editions with some minor differences to the criteria. The *DSM-5* brings no changes to the first two criteria from the *DSM-IV-TR*. These criteria are repeated, uncontrollable binge eating episodes accompanied by ongoing compensatory behaviors to avoid weight gain, including self-induced vomiting; misuse of laxatives, diuretics, or other medications; fasting; or excessive exercise. Also unchanged in the new edition is the fourth criterion, the following key cognitive symptom: self-evaluation is unduly influenced by body shape and weight. The major change to BN in the *DSM-5* is in the third criterion, the frequency of the compensatory behaviors. In the *DSM-5*, the frequency of compensatory behaviors has been reduced from an average of twice weekly to an average of only once per week. The three-month duration remains the same, though. A secondary change to the BN criteria is related to the purging and nonpurging specifiers. In the past, these specifiers described the type of compensatory behavior used by the individual, but these have been eliminated because they have been deemed unnecessary. Similar to the other eating disorders, BN has severity specifiers now.

For this diagnosis, the assessment of severity depends upon the average number of times purging occurs in a given week. Depending on the frequency of compensatory behaviors each week, a case may be categorized as one the following: extreme (14 or more episodes), severe (8–13 episodes), moderate (4–7 episodes), and mild (1–3 episodes). Finally, as with other disorders in the *DSM-5*, specifiers of partial or full remission can be applied to the diagnosis.

Binge Eating Disorder

The diagnosis of BED is new to the *DSM-5*. First mentioned in the *DSM-IV*, binge eating appeared in that edition and the subsequent text revision under "Eating Disorder Not Otherwise Specified," with research criteria outlined in "Appendix B: Criteria Sets and Axes Provided for Further Study." BED shares the binge eating criterion of BN (i.e., consuming a relatively large quantity of food in a short period of time while experiencing a loss of control). The primary distinction from BN is that individuals with BED do not engage in compensatory behaviors after binge eating. An additional difference is that BED does not include the criterion related to an undue influence of weight and shape on self-concept. The second criterion for BED includes five items and specifies that individuals must display a minimum of three to qualify for diagnosis. These criteria are related to behaviors, emotions, and cognitions associated with binge eating. For example, eating in the absence of physical hunger, eating unusually quickly, and experiencing feelings of guilt and disgust around eating. Although a diagnosis of BN requires the presence of binge eating, the BN diagnosis does not include these additional criteria. Comparable to other feeding and eating disorders, the diagnostic criteria for BED in the *DSM-5* shows a decrease in the duration and frequency requirements. While the research criteria in the *DSM-IV-TR* suggested that bingeing must occur at least two days a week for six months, the *DSM-5* suggests the diagnostic criteria are met if the binge eating occurs an average of once per week for a minimum of three months. Aligned with the other eating disorders, *DSM-5* includes a severity specifier for BED, with between one and three episodes per week constituting mild BED and 14 or more episodes per week qualifying as extreme.

Obesity

The introduction to the chapter on feeding and eating disorders explicitly addresses the decision not to include obesity as a diagnosis in the *DSM-5*, suggesting that obesity develops from a combination of genetic, physiological, behavioral, and environmental factors that varies across individuals and is the result of an excess of energy intake relative to energy expenditure over the course of a long period of time. Simply stated, obesity is a physical condition, not a psychological state. The introduction goes on to clarify, however, that there exists a complicated relationship between obesity and several psychiatric conditions—particularly feeding and eating disorders.

Other Specified Feeding or Eating Disorder and Unspecified Feeding or Eating Disorder

The *DSM*-IV-TR wrapped up the section of eating disorders with the diagnostic category of "Eating Disorder Not Otherwise Specified (EDNOS)," but this category was eliminated from the *DSM*-5. The EDNOS category was previously reserved for individuals who did not meet the criteria for AN or BN (e.g., a woman who meets criteria for AN except that she has regular menses), but, anecdotally, it was overused by medical providers. According to research, nearly 60 percent of individuals being treated by a medical provider were assigned this diagnosis.

In addition to updated criteria and new diagnoses, there are two new diagnostic categories that replaced EDNOS: other specified feeding or eating disorder (OSFED) and unspecified feeding or eating disorder. Similar to EDNOS, OSFED continues to represent individuals who present symptoms characteristic of a feeding or eating disorder that causes clinically significant impairment, but who do not meet the full criteria for any of the disorders in this section. However, when assigning this diagnosis, the provider is able to specify or state the specific reason that the presentation does not meet the full criteria. Thus the specific reason should follow the diagnosis. If individuals meet all of the criteria of BN except that the inappropriate compensatory behavior and binge eating occur at a frequency less than once a week and/or for less than three months, they could be assigned the OSFED diagnosis with BN (of low frequency and/or limited duration).

This diagnosis presents a contrast with another new diagnosis, unspecified feeding or eating disorder, where the provider is unable to provide the specific reason why the presentation or the eating disorder does not meet full criteria. In this case, the client would be displaying symptoms of an eating or feeding disorder that is causing clinically significant impairment, but there was insufficient information from the client to diagnose due to treatment occurring in an emergency setting or the provider failing to gather enough information during the intake.

EATING DISORDER ASSESSMENT

Early detection, initial evaluation, and effective treatment are important steps that can help an individual with an eating disorder move into recovery more quickly, preventing the disorder from progressing to a more severe or chronic state. According to the National Eating Disorders Association (NEDA), "the following assessments are recommended as the first steps to diagnosis and will help determine the level of care needed." Receiving appropriate treatment is the first step toward recovery.

Patient Assessment

In order to diagnose an eating disorder and determine the treatment moving forward, NEDA has recommended the following types of questions: "patient history including screening questions about eating patterns, determination of medical, nutritional, psychological and social functioning, attitudes towards eating, exercise, and appearance, family history of eating disorder or other psychiatric disorder, including alcohol and substance use disorders, family history of obesity, and assessment of other mental health conditions, such as depression and anxiety."

Medical Exam

Eating disorders are often accompanied by medical issues that can result from binge eating, self-starvation, overexercise, and other compensatory methods. Therefore, an evaluation by a qualified medical professional is an essential part of ED treatment. NEDA has established that a medical professional should evaluate the following: "physical examination including height, weight, body mass index (BMI), growth chart assessment for children and adolescents, cardiovascular and peripheral vascular function, skin health, hair loss, evidence of self-injurious behaviors, measurement of body temperature and pulse, orthostatic blood pressure, laboratory tests, dental exam if self-induced vomiting is known or suspected, and the diagnosis and recommendations for an appropriate level of care."

Laboratory Testing

A variety of laboratory tests and blood work may be needed to determine the most appropriate ED diagnosis and assess the appropriate level of care for an individual. NEDA has confirmed that the laboratory tests should evaluate the following types of factors: "blood sugar levels, electrolyte levels, to determine the presence and severity of dehydration, especially if someone is purging, liver and kidney functioning, chemicals in the urine, electrocardiogram (ECG), which ensures the heart is beating properly." NEDA has the most comprehensive list available of laboratory tests and details about what the laboratory tests might be testing for.

DIFFERENTIAL DIAGNOSES

Differential diagnosis is the process of differentiating between two or more diagnoses that share similar signs or symptoms. All of the feeding and eating disorders have differential diagnoses laid out in the *DSM-5* to consider.

Pica

According to the *DSM-5*, one of the differential diagnoses for pica is AN. Pica can usually be differentiated from the other eating disorders because it includes the consumption of nonnutritive, nonfood substances (e.g., tissues, cotton balls, dirt). It is important to remember that AN should be the primary diagnosis if the individual is ingesting nonnutritive, nonfood substances as a means to control appetite or weight. Another differential diagnosis for pica is factitious disorder. Some individuals diagnosed with factitious disorder may intentionally ingest nonnutritive, nonfood substances in order to produce physical symptoms. Finally, some individuals diagnosed with personality disorders may ingest potentially nonnutritive, nonfood substances in order to self-harm or as part of a maladaptive behavior.

Rumination

For rumination, gastrointestinal conditions are often differential diagnoses according to the *DSM-5*. It is important to differentiate the regurgitation symptom in rumination disorder from other illnesses with vomiting or acid reflux. The *DSM-5* suggests that conditions such as gastroparesis, pyloric stenosis, hiatal hernia, and Sandifer syndrome in infants should be eliminated with laboratory tests and physical examinations. AN and BN are also differential diagnoses for rumination disorder—especially when an individual is engaging in regurgitating or spitting out food as a way of getting rid of it.

Avoidant/Restrictive Food Intake Disorder

According to the *DSM-5*, it is important to note that ARFID can be diagnosed as comorbid with a number of medical and mental disorders if all criteria are met and the eating disturbance requires specific clinical attention, but it can also be mistaken for other diagnoses. Appetite loss prior to restricting food intake is a common symptom that can accompany a plethora of medical conditions. ARFID is often mistaken for medical conditions such as food allergies and intolerances, gastrointestinal disease, or even cancer. Food restriction may also take place in other medical conditions, especially those with ongoing symptoms such as loss of appetite, nausea, vomiting, abdominal pain, and diarrhea. A diagnosis of ARFID necessitates that the disturbance of food intake be greater than what would be reasonably expected with a specific medical condition and that symptoms persist after the medical condition has resolved. There are also some neurological and neuromuscular as well as structural and congenital disorders and conditions associated with eating issues that are often comorbid and/or differential diagnoses for ARFID. As for mental health disorders, ARFID also has a number of differential diagnoses according to the *DSM-5*. Reactive attachment disorder, a disorder where an infant or young child does not establish healthy attachments with parents or other caregivers, can also be a differential diagnosis for ARFID. Specific phobia, other type, includes situations that could lead to vomiting or choking that triggers anxiety, fear, or avoidance. Specific phobia can be difficult to tell apart from ARFID when a fear of vomiting or choking results in avoiding food. Although avoidance or restriction of food secondary to fears could be diagnosed as specific phobia, in situations where the eating issues become the primary focus of clinical attention, ARFID would be the best diagnosis. In social anxiety disorder and ARFID, an individual might be worried about being watched by others, and social anxiety disorder would be considered a differential diagnosis. With regard to AN as a differential diagnosis, individuals with AN will typically show a fear of weight gain or will show behaviors that interfere with weight gain as well as a misperception and experience of their own body shape or size, while individuals with ARFID will not show these thoughts and behaviors. Notably, ARFID and AN should not be diagnosed concurrently. An individual with obsessive-compulsive disorder (OCD) might avoid foods in service of their obsessions or compulsions, so ARFID would be diagnosed concurrently only if all criteria are met for both disorders and the eating issues are a focus of clinical attention. In major depressive disorder, appetite could be impacted to the point that food intake is restricted and weight loss occurs. Fortunately, appetite loss and reduced food intake often improve when the mood disorder resolves. According to the *DSM-5*, ARFID should only be used concurrently if full criteria are met for both disorders and when the eating issues require intervention. Individuals with schizophrenia, delusional disorder, or other psychotic disorders may exhibit odd eating behaviors or avoid specific foods due to delusions or hallucinations, but ARFID should be diagnosed concurrently only if all criteria are met for both disorders and when the eating issues require intervention. In order to assume the sick role, an individual with factitious disorder might embellish how restrictive a diet is or the complications of that restriction. In factitious disorder imposed on another, the caregiver could also describe symptoms consistent with ARFID and might induce physical symptoms such as failure to gain weight. These would be important factors to consider when examining factitious disorder as a potential diagnosis.

Anorexia Nervosa

For differential diagnosis with AN, other possible causes of significant weight loss or significantly low body weight should be considered—especially when the presenting features are atypical (e.g., onset after 40 years of age) according to the *DSM-5*. AN can also be confused with many medical conditions (e.g., hypothyroidism, gastrointestinal disease, cancer, and acquired immunodeficiency syndrome [AIDS]). In major depressive disorder, severe weight loss may occur, but most individuals with major depressive disorder do not have either an intense fear of gaining weight or a desire for excessive weight loss. An individual with schizophrenia may occasionally experience significant weight loss or exhibit odd eating behavior but will rarely show fear around weight gain and does not tend to body image disturbances. An individual with a substance use disorder will often experience low weight due to poor nutrition but generally does not have body image issues or fear of gaining weight. An individual who abuses substances that reduce appetite (e.g., stimulants) and who also fears gaining weight should be cautiously assessed for AN since the substance could be the mechanism to control weight. Some of the features of AN overlap with the criteria for social phobia, OCD, and body dysmorphic disorder. An individual with BN might experience repeated episodes of binge eating, engage in compensatory behaviors to avoid weight gain (e.g., self-induced vomiting), and be overly concerned with body shape and weight but tend to maintain a body weight at or above a minimally normal level, unlike individuals with AN, binge eating/purging type.

Bulimia Nervosa

According to the *DSM-5*, individuals should not be diagnosed with BN if their binge eating behaviors only occur during AN episodes. An individual who binges and purges, was initially diagnosed with AN, but no longer meets criteria for AN—typically because the person's weight has normalized—should not be diagnosed with BN until all criteria for BN have been met for at least three months. If an individual is bingeing regularly, but the person's utilization of compensatory behaviors is irregular, a diagnosis of BED should be considered. In certain neurological or other medical conditions, there are often eating issues and even purging, but the characteristic psychological features of BN, such as concern with body size and shape, do not exist. Bingeing is often common with major depressive disorder, but an individual will not typically engage in compensatory behaviors and will not be overly concerned with body size or shape. Both diagnoses can be given if criteria for both disorders are present. Bingeing is often one of the behaviors included with borderline personality disorder, and borderline personality disorder can be diagnosed with BN if criteria for both are present.

Binge Eating Disorder

According to the *DSM*-5, BED has recurrent binge eating comparable to BN but is distinct in a few ways. Most notably, the compensatory behaviors (e.g., purging, laxative use, overexercise) are completely absent in BED. Individuals with BED do not typically engage in any compensatory behaviors that would influence their body size or shape. Weight gain and increased appetite are included in the criteria for a major depressive episode and in the atypical feature specifiers for depressive and bipolar disorders, but the increased appetite during a major depressive episode may or may not be associated with loss of control. If the full criteria for BED and the depressive or bipolar disorders are met, both diagnoses can be given. As mentioned with BN, bingeing is often one of the behaviors included with borderline personality disorder, and borderline personality disorder can be diagnosed with BED if criteria for both are present.

EMPIRICALLY SUPPORTED TREATMENTS FOR EATING DISORDERS

There are numerous treatments or therapies for eating disorders, but they have varying levels of research to support their use. According to NEDA, an empirically supported treatment or therapy is "the conscientious, explicit and judicious use of current best evidence in making decisions about the care of individual patients." Empirically supported treatments have typically been researched and believed to be effective in reducing symptoms of an eating disorder. Classifying a treatment as empirically supported does not mean that it will work for everyone, just that it works for some individuals with the diagnosis. It is also important to understand that some treatment providers who utilize an empirically supported treatment might not use it in all of their sessions. For example, treatment providers might primarily work through a psychodynamic lens but use some interventions based in cognitive-behavioral therapy.

NEDA has identified a list of empirically supported treatments or therapies frequently utilized with individuals with eating disorders.

Acceptance and Commitment Therapy

Acceptance and commitment therapy (ACT) is focused on changing actions as opposed to changing feelings or thoughts. An individual is encouraged to identify core values and commit to developing goals that align with these values. ACT also aims to inspire an individual to distance themselves from feelings and thoughts and work to understand that pain is an essential part of life. The goal of ACT is not to be comfortable or feel better but to live an authentic life. Coincidentally, through living an authentic life, individuals will often find themselves starting to feel better.

Dialectical Behavior Therapy

Dialectical Behavior Therapy (DBT) is geared toward changing behaviors. With eating disorders, treatment is focused on developing coping skills to replace maladaptive disordered eating behaviors. These skills focus on mindfulness, emotion regulation, distress tolerance, and interpersonal effectiveness. Although DBT was initially developed to treat borderline personality disorder, it is becoming more popular in the treatment of eating disorders.

Cognitive Behavioral Therapy and Enhanced Cognitive Behavioral Therapy

According to NEDA, cognitive behavioral therapy (CBT) and enhanced cognitive behavioral therapy (CBT-E) is "a relatively short-term, symptom-oriented therapy focusing on the beliefs, values, and cognitive processes that maintain the eating disorder behavior. It aims to modify distorted beliefs and attitudes about the meaning of weight, shape, and appearance, which are correlated to the development and maintenance of the eating disorder."

Cognitive Remediation Therapy

Also according to NEDA, cognitive remediation therapy (CRT) focuses on "developing the ability of an individual to focus on more than one thing." The therapy targets "rigid thinking processes . . . believed to be a core component of AN through simple exercises, reflection, and guided supervision."

Family-Based Treatment

Family-based treatment (FBT) or the Maudsley Method/Approach is a occurs in the home and is shown to be effective with adolescents diagnosed with AN and BN. FBT focuses on refeeding and weight restoration in order to eventually address the origin of the eating disorder. All family members are necessary to restore weight and interrupt ED behaviors before returning control of eating back to the adolescent and tackling underlying issues after weight has been restored.

Psychodynamic Psychotherapy

The psychodynamic approach demands that recovery is only possible if the origin of the eating disorder is addressed. According to NEDA, psychodynamic psychotherapists look at ED behaviors as "the result of internal conflicts, motives and unconscious forces, and if behaviors are discontinued without addressing the underlying causes that are driving them, then inevitably relapse will occur." Symptoms are also seen as "expressions of the patient's underlying needs and issues and are thought to be resolved with the completion of working through these issues."

LEVELS OF CARE

ED treatment is provided at varying levels of care. Understanding the different levels of care is important when moving forward with treatment. Established by the American Psychiatric Association, the list below is ordered from the least intensive treatment options to the most intensive treatment options.

Outpatient Treatment and Intensive Outpatient Treatment

For outpatient and intensive outpatient treatments, an individual must be medically stable and not need daily medical monitoring. The individual must also be psychiatrically stable and have any ED symptoms under control to be able to function in social, educational, or vocational situations. The individual must also be willing to continue to make progress in recovery. According to NEDA, "many individuals with eating disorders respond to outpatient therapy, including individual, group or family therapy, and medical management by their primary care provider. Support groups, nutrition counseling and psychiatric medications administered under careful medical supervision have also proven helpful for some individuals."

Partial Hospitalization Treatment

For treatment by partial hospitalization, an individual is medically stable, but the ED symptoms are impairing functioning—although there is no immediate risk—and daily assessment of physiologic and mental status is needed. An individual is also psychiatrically stable but is unable to function in social, educational, or vocational situations. This individual might be engaging in regular restricting or bingeing behaviors as well as compensatory behaviors.

Residential Treatment

For residential treatment, an individual is medically stable and requires no intensive medical intervention (e.g., feeding tube). This individual is likely psychiatrically impaired and unable to respond to lower levels of care.

Inpatient Treatment

In inpatient treatment, an individual is medically unstable as determined by vital signs, laboratory reports, and complications due to co-occurring medical problems (e.g., diabetes). The individual is also psychiatrically unstable as evidenced by worsening symptoms or suicidality. Inpatient treatment will require follow-up at lower levels of care to address the origin or underlying issues related to the eating disorder.

Regardless of the level of care, an individual with an eating disorder is best served by a multidisciplinary team that may include a therapist (e.g., licensed psychologist, licensed professional counselor, licensed marriage and family therapist, or licensed social worker), dietician or nutritionist, psychiatrist, and/or primary care physician. Care should be coordinated and provided by a health professional with expertise and experience in managing eating disorders.

TREATMENT OF COMORBID DIAGNOSES AND CONDITIONS

A number of the feeding and eating disorders are often comorbid (occurring at the same time) with other diagnoses and/or conditions.

Pica

Pica is most commonly comorbid with autism spectrum disorder and intellectual disabilities and, to a lesser degree, schizophrenia and OCD. Pica can also be associated with trichotillomania (hair-pulling disorder) and excoriation (skin-picking) disorder. In comorbid presentations for trichotillomania and excoriation, the hair or skin is typically ingested. Pica can also be comorbid with ARFID, particularly with individuals who have a strong sensory component to their presentation. When an individual is known to have pica, assessment should include consideration of the possibility of gastrointestinal complications, poisoning, infection, and nutritional deficiency.

Rumination

Regurgitation with comorbid rumination can occur in the context of a concurrent medical condition or another mental disorder (e.g., generalized anxiety disorder). When the regurgitation occurs in this context, a diagnosis of rumination disorder is appropriate only when the severity of the disturbance exceeds that routinely associated with such conditions or disorders and warrants additional clinical attention.

Avoidant/Restrictive Intake Food Disorder

The most commonly observed disorders comorbid with ARFID are anxiety disorders, OCD, and neurodevelopmental disorders (specifically, autism spectrum disorder, attention-deficit/hyperactivity disorder, and intellectual disability [intellectual developmental disorder]).

Anorexia Nervosa

Bipolar, depressive, and anxiety disorders are commonly comorbid with AN. Individuals with AN often report the presence of either an anxiety disorder or symptoms of anxiety prior to onset of their eating disorder. OCD is often diagnosed in some individuals with AN, especially those with the restricting type. Alcohol use disorder and other substance use disorders may also be comorbid with AN, especially among those with the binge eating/purging type.

Bulimia Nervosa

BN tends to have more comorbidity than other eating disorders. Most individuals diagnosed with BN experience at least one other mental disorder and many will experience multiple comorbidities. With BN, there is an increased frequency of depressive symptoms (e.g., low self-esteem) and bipolar and depressive disorders are often comorbid. Despite BN being blamed on the mood disturbance, the mood disturbance often begins at the same time as, or follows the development of, BN. Occasionally, the mood disturbance can precede the development of BN, but it is rarer. There may also be an increased frequency of anxiety symptoms (e.g., fear of social situations) or anxiety disorders. These mood and anxiety disturbances frequently resolve following effective treatment of BN. The lifetime prevalence of substance use, particularly alcohol or stimulant use, is at least 30 percent among individuals with BN. Stimulant use often begins in an attempt to control appetite and weight. A substantial percentage of individuals with BN also have personality features that meet criteria for one or more personality disorders, most frequently borderline personality disorder.

Binge Eating Disorder

BED is comorbid with several mental disorders comparable to the ones that are comorbid with BN and AN. The most common comorbid disorders are depressive disorders, bipolar disorders, anxiety disorders, and, sometimes, substance use disorders. The psychiatric comorbidity is linked to the severity of binge eating and not to the degree of obesity.

Now that more about ED diagnosis and treatment is understood, the next chapter will dive into the long-term prognosis and potential complications associated with an eating disorder.

6

Long-Term Prognosis and Potential Complications

Recovering from an eating disorder can be a long and exhausting process with multiple phases. All individuals are different with regard to how they respond to treatment and support, which makes a clear-cut treatment protocol or plan impossible to define. Treatment is customized to individual needs and does not guarantee a full recovery. Unfortunately, most individuals struggling with an eating disorder experience at least one form of regression or relapse with behavior patterns, even after experiencing phases of full recovery and a symptom-free life for long periods of time. Some are unable to rebound at all and end up spending a lifetime in what is described as a *chronic* eating disorder. A chronic eating disorder and its prognosis also entail a different type of therapy and structure in order to help one maintain medical stability while continuously or intermittently engaging in ED behaviors. As expected, this course includes a combination of physical, emotional, psychological, and interpersonal consequences that can change the direction of a person's life and, at times, have lethal outcomes. An eating disorder can also be a slow progression of suicide in itself. Suicidality, often in conjunction with a depressive mood presentation, is closely associated with the mortality of eating disorders. The positive news is that there are many signs one can be aware of and ways to seek help, or help someone else, if this becomes a concern for a family member, a coworker, or a friend.

Current research and exploration looking at changes in the brain have shed greater light on the impact this organ has in conjunction with an eating disorder, as well as how the brain is influenced by specific types of behaviors. Observed changes in the brain have led to much more detailed approaches in conceptualizing an eating disorder and more variety of treatment options, and they have provided an understanding into the possible predisposition of the development of an eating disorder.

SLIPS, LAPSES, AND RELAPSES

Many researchers have included large numbers of participants in long-term studies focusing on relapse rates. However, detecting differences between the various types of eating disorders based on setbacks or periods of regression has been complicated. This is partly due to the changing criteria for each type of eating disorder as versions of the *DSM* have been repeatedly updated over the years. Findings also suggest consistent variability of symptoms, and, consequently, the specific type of eating disorder diagnosed can change throughout the duration of one's battle.

With regard to anorexia, studies vary in specifying the rates of relapse. A 2013 study at the University of Toronto suggested a broader range than most, between 9 and 65 percent, while Berends and colleagues' more recent findings note a 35 to 41 percent relapse rate for those with anorexia, even after sustaining time in remission. Typically, the most common time period of relapse occurs between 4 and 17 months after completing treatment. A more recent study by Stice, Marti, and Rohde (2013) looked at relapse rates utilizing *DSM*-5 criteria and found a 25 percent recurrence rate for anorexia, 23 percent for bulimia, and 33 percent for binge eating disorder. Another complicating factor when it comes to narrowing in on relapse rates is the significant inconsistencies in those who only reach partial recovery.

Slips, *lapses*, and *relapses* are a few of the terms used when describing difficulty maintaining, or regressing, with regard to ED behaviors. These can occur at various expected and unexpected points in one's journey. Often, stepping into a lower level of care sparks challenges in sustaining improvement and shifts without a corresponding amount of support and structure. It can be daunting to consistently reach out for the necessary amount of support in the face of recovery when one is challenged to seek support independently or with less accountability. This, of course, will depend on what level of care one started with and ended at as well. Unexpected life events, loss, location change, or interpersonal challenges can also trigger a regression in some form. How one reacts is one of the more distinguishable differences between a slip, lapse, and relapse.

A slip is when one experiences a deviation from a recovery-focused routine, meal plan, exercise regimen, or even change in perception of these specific components, often with some level of awareness. This is frequently in response to a distorted or irrational eating-disordered belief. Contrary to a lapse or relapse, someone who experiences a slip is able to rebound from this urge or even slight behavioral change without significant alterations in the recovery process. Slips can be important to experience in order to build evidence and belief that although recovery is not in the form of a perfect straight line, the individual does have the tools to respond effectively.

A lapse is more pronounced and longer lasting than a slip; however, the person is still able to rebound and get back on track with recovery. An example might be giving into an urge to binge but catching oneself midbehavior and shortening the amount of time spent in the behavior or lessening the amount of food consumed. Someone struggling with overexercise, may recognize a pull to go faster or complete longer distances while running but is able to discontinue this behavior before completing the run. If someone is able to revert back to a recovery track after one or a few of these behaviors, this is more in line with a lapse. As mentioned before, recovery is not flawless or a complete deviation from struggle. However, if approached with awareness and grace, it can provide helpful reminders and information about the more challenging scenarios or environments that could potentially instigate multiple lapses or eventually a full relapse.

Reflection and awareness of the behavior are important distinguishing factors for a lapse because they determine one's ability to not make these choices repeatedly. In this case, the person may be moving closer to a relapse, hence the term *relapse* referring to multiple lapses. A relapse means the person again meets full criteria for a type of eating disorder, which is often assessed and diagnosed by a professional. A partial relapse is the redevelopment of a few, but not all, defining symptoms. Often there is fluctuation with behaviors and symptoms, which can change the diagnosis. Differentiating between these two can also be done by looking at one's ability to interrupt these behaviors with various types of support or therapeutic intervention put into place. While a relapse can feel defeating, it is not uncommon. It also provides the opportunity to complete a different type of work during another round of treatment or more intense therapy.

Predictors of Relapse

When it comes to predicting the outcome of an eating disorder, there is little relationship between anorexia and binge eating disorder but more common links between anorexia and bulimia. This has also been observed between bulimia and binge eating disorder. This would imply the potential for similar psychological factors that maintain the ED behaviors among these types, including the occurrence of mood disorder symptoms or diagnoses such as depression or anxiety. Crossover is most common in presentations involving binge eating behaviors. There is also a common intersection between the two subtypes of anorexia, restrictive type and binge eating/purging-type.

With regard to predictors for relapse, there are both similarities and differences among specific types of eating disorders. While studying predictors of relapse in those recovering from bulimia, Olmsted, MacDonald, McFarlane, Trottier, and Colton (2015) found that those who relapsed engaged in more frequent binge-purge episodes before beginning their episode of treatment. Additionally, those who had a slower response to treatment also experienced less body avoidance. This outcome contradicts other findings that have found poor body image to be one of the more significant predictors of relapse.

According to Berends and colleagues' work (2016), length of stay in treatment, as well as the specific level of treatment, may also be influential in predicting one's outcome or susceptibility to regression to ED behaviors after treatment. This also requires taking into account the reasons for the amount of time spent in treatment, which could signify the severity level of the eating disorder itself. If one was already in an outpatient setting, the relapse rate would most likely be lower, considering the individual's ability to be practicing recovery at the outpatient level in the first place. Those older than 19 years of age were also observed to be more prone to relapse.

Preventing Relapse

There are many precautions one can take in order to prevent and plan for situations that could lead to a relapse. A structured aftercare plan that includes lower level of care options and support is essential. Preferably, those involved throughout the duration of one's treatment would be crucial components to a post-treatment and accountability support system due to their familiarity and knowledge. While one may feel ready to step into life in recovery on one's own after treatment, or even with some level of structured environment with support, many unknowns and obstacles will likely arise at some point. It is vital that all individuals are made aware of the high potential for relapse during the first few months but also in the time following, as the possibility extends way beyond this time period. Berends and colleagues' study (2016) highly suggests that intervention as soon as possible, ideally within one week of a slip or lapse occurring, is crucial for preventing a full-blown relapse. Intervention would include contacting one or more professional members of the aftercare or outpatient team in order to plan accordingly and make necessary changes specific to the individual's needs. While each person is different with regard to treatment needs, the composition of an outpatient team often includes an individual therapist, dietician, and psychiatrist, the latter if medication management is necessary. Additional support, such as a family therapist, therapy group, and a primary care physician who is familiar with eating disorders, is also commonly utilized. If possible, overlapping one's sessions in between treatment settings can prevent time gaps lacking in support or accountability. Before stepping down into a lower level of care or outpatient setting, communication and shared information about an individual's work in treatment, including successful coping strategies, are essential between providers and conducive to enduring a smoother transition. A significant component of one's relapse-prevention planning is acknowledging and discussing the high potential for relapse. Thoroughly assessing one's risk and planning accordingly in order not to return to behaviors is beneficial, especially in the initial stages.

While it is important to be there for someone in the midst of an untreated illness, or when the person is seeking help for it, it is equally as beneficial to be aware of signs of potential relapse. They can provide useful information regarding how and when to intervene. Cockell, Zaitsoff, and Geller (2004) highlight the importance of familial and social support when it comes to helping someone sustain recovery. This preventive measure for one's relapse is most effective when the members of one's support system approach and treat the individual with an acceptance and grace for where at the individual is situated on the journey, which can vary from person to person, depending on readiness and motivation for change. Cockell, Zaitsoff, and Geller also mention the importance of helping someone find space away from the eating disorder identity by encouraging a different routine or participation in activities not connected to being sick. An example would be returning to work or a volunteer opportunity that exemplifies normalcy around food and provides interpersonal connection. Another great source of support is connecting with others who have been through recovery themselves and can relate in a very direct way. Frequent check-ins, communication, and a place to ask questions or express curiosities with someone familiar with the recovery process is a very useful outlet and can instill a sense of inspiration and empowerment. On the flip side, it has been shown that when a lack of support or insensitivity to one's needs for recovery is present, relapse is more likely to occur.

THE CHRONIC NATURE OF EATING DISORDERS

The term *chronic* is used in reference to the expression of an eating disorder that has not responded to initial rounds of treatment. Unfortunately, the behaviors evolve into an unrelenting and continuous cycle for a significant period of time in one's life. The severity and frequency of symptoms shift but never fully subside. The conceptualization and treatment approach from the clinicians in helping positions mirror these shifts in order to make the goal more aligned with stability and maintenance of symptoms instead of full remission.

Chronicity should be evaluated on more than just the length of time one spends in the illness. Other factors to consider may include the clinical level of ED behaviors themselves, the amount of time spent in previous ED treatment programs or facilities, and the individual's response to the treatment interventions implemented. Additionally, observation around the level to which one's individual functioning is impacted is important. This would include medical, psychological, familial, professional, and interpersonal levels of functioning, which are all very important to think through when categorizing an eating disorder as chronic.

Long, Fitzgerald, and Hollin (2012) evaluated 34 adults who were clinically diagnosed with anorexia, either the restrictive type or the binge-purge type. These patients were followed for four years beginning in the acute phase of inpatient treatment through outpatient levels of care. Observation included keeping an eye on the maintenance of their weight restoration as well as follow-up meetings. The content of the follow-ups entailed completion of various assessments that evaluated factors such as ED symptoms, mood presentation, body image thoughts, and level of body satisfaction. The use of specific assessment measures in their study revealed that those who entered remission continued to improve on the comprehensive collection of assessments administered, while those who relapsed never improved on some measures at all. This specifically included body dissatisfaction and interpersonal distrust scales. These individuals also struggled to make progress with sustaining a normal BMI, while those who entered remission were able to improve and maintain a BMI within the normal range.

Protective Factors for the Chronicity of an Eating Disorder

When it comes to predicting relapse, researchers have looked into specific factors as well as differences among types of eating disorders. For example, Long, Fitzgerald, and Hollin team found that a higher number of participants with anorexia binge-purge type recovered, compared to those categorized as restrictive type. It is important to consider what separates those who relapse from those who remain in recovery. Specific aspects that have been shown to improve chances of long-term remission include improved psychological mood, better body image perception, decreased distress, practice and incorporation of effective coping skills, consistent attendance with outpatient appointments, and readiness and willingness for change. This final factor is key when we think about one's internal motivation and drive to commit to what is required for getting better for any amount of time. Mander, Teufel, Keifenheim, Zipfel, and Giel (2013) looked at the relationship between stages of change in those suffering from chronic anorexia and long-term treatment outcome. There is a strong correlation between ambivalence regarding commitment to change and severe malnourishment resulting in low weight. When a physical body is starved, the brain is as well, which makes decision-making surrounding readiness for change even more difficult than it already is. The *maintenance* stage within Prochaska and DiClemente's Transtheoretical Model represents the phase of working to maintain change in order to prevent regression. In Mander et al.'s research, this stage was the only one that revealed a strong correlation with relapse rates. This would imply that the difficulty associated with sustaining changes made in treatment can lead to chronicity as the individual repeatedly engages in the same pattern with less support and structure.

Treatment of Chronic Eating Disorders

Unfortunately, there is little empirically based research, or research that is based on observation, that supports one recommendation or approach over another for treating a chronic eating disorder. This may be because the terms and descriptions of "chronic" fluctuate due to vastly varying clinical presentations as well as differences among clinicians' interpretation.

Wonderlich and colleagues' (2012) thorough review of treatment approaches for chronic eating disorders sheds light on the varied perspectives that clinicians may choose when working with someone who has been battling this illness without much improvement. Some clinicians take a more firm and direct approach with the intention of potentially influencing a shift in one's attitude toward recovery, while others take a less resistant stance in an effort to join the individual where that individual is. Ultimately, establishing trust in the process, maintaining consistent boundaries from the beginning, and avoiding additional control wars, especially since this is already occurring internally for the person with the illness, will ideally lead to less resistance toward treatment altogether.

As many approaches and settings are often not effective in the long term and contribute to developing a chronic illness, Wonderlich et al.'s (2012) review also suggests setting specific guidelines to aid in the treatment of a chronic eating disorder. These may include, but are not limited to, components such as maintenance of appropriate weight ranges, higher level of care options when necessary, a required commitment level, and contract-type documents confirming agreement from all involved. This planning would likely include the individual's support system in order to maintain therapeutic effectiveness with a team-centered approach.

Yager (1992) also recommends involvement from family or key support members. The intention would be to acquire not just additional support but also information from them regarding what has or has not worked in the past with regard to particular treatment settings or approaches. This could help in jointly setting realistic and agreed-upon goals for the individual's work ahead.

While the therapeutic approach may differ among clinicians, all will agree that monitoring medical stability and intervening with a higher level of care when needed is critical. Outpatient, hospital-based, or a combination of both will also be considered, depending on the necessity of medical stability for each person. A professional team of support could possibly include a case manager or social worker, primary care physician, outpatient individual therapist, family therapist, psychiatrist, and therapeutic support groups. Additionally, a connection with a hospital setting for immediate stabilization for specific needs including dehydration, abnormal labs, or electrolyte imbalances is also imperative. The amount of time and frequency spent with each or any of these providers is typically determined by the team, depending on individual needs.

The harm-reduction approach is another framework for treating chronic addictions and disorders, including eating disorders. This method aims at minimizing symptoms as much as possible in order to treat the medical and psychological consequences of having an eating disorder for a long period of time. It also concentrates on improving individuals' quality of life. One of the main priorities is keeping the affected persons medically steady and planning for brief interventions when they need a higher level of care or hospitalization for stabilization. It can be helpful to use information from previous treatment settings in order to adjust a treatment plan accordingly.

It is important to help persons who are struggling find some level of stability in order to function on a daily basis, as well as to find joy and meaning in their everyday activities, responsibilities, and relationships. One example of this is another resource highlighted in Wonderlich et al.'s review (2012), the Community Outreach Partnership Program (COPP). While there are expectations and guidelines for participating in this program, COPP utilizes motivational interviewing techniques to help individuals develop a strong community of support when traditional treatment programs have not been successful. The aim is to improve quality of life and autonomy, while contact with the team of clinicians is less formal and does not always take place in a treatment-type setting. The COPP framework has shown improvement among its participants in interpersonal, mood, and ED dimensions.

While it is difficult to watch someone choose to stay within an illness on some level, acceptance and respect for the person's particular level of readiness or willingness to explore change is essential in building trust and being able to also effectively implement and maintain boundaries. Vitousek and colleagues (1998) reflect a similar sentiment in the sense of encouraging motivational change but not making this the primary goal. Others, including Robinson (2009), encourage viewing a chronic eating disorder as a severe and enduring eating disorder (SEED). He compared this to other critical psychiatric disorders and suggested implementing a framework similar to psychiatric rehabilitation. This would include focus around overall self-care, quality of life assessment, and multiple treatment team members from different domains.

CHANGES IN THE BRAIN

While the number is relatively low, there have been studies and investigations utilizing advanced brain-imaging techniques to look at the connection and influence between eating disorders and the brain. Guido Frank, a board-certified psychiatrist, has published valuable research highlighting what has been studied and learned in recent years, specifically involving information about brain circuits, behaviors, reward function, and neurological pathways. These findings have provided greater knowledge about the influence ED behaviors may have on the brain, as well as how one's brain could impact the development of an eating disorder. The hope is that these advancements will eventually aid in treatment planning and, ultimately, improve chances of recovery.

In his 2016 book, *What Causes Eating Disorders—And What Do They Cause?*, Guido Frank shared that different behaviors, specifically, restriction, binge-purging, and overeating, have been associated with varying levels of motivation surrounding the necessary amount of food intake for a human. These motivational differences can increase the frequency of particular ED patterns. For example, individuals struggling with anorexia have demonstrated less drive when it comes to fueling their body appropriately, which leads to consuming a lower amount of food than is needed to survive.

Researchers have also observed a change in brain volume, specifically gray and white matter, when one restricts or overeats. Dahlberg et al.'s (2017) research is an example of this in adolescents with anorexia, while earlier research has focused on adults. Their results further correlated these changes in brain volume with shifts in cognition and working memory. Fuglet and her team (2013) also confirmed a similar idea in their respective case studies. They found that portions of the brain may be vulnerable to restriction and suggest a link to the physiological processes of an eating disorder. It has been recommended that future research investigate whether or not changes in the brain are a cause or an outcome of an eating disorder.

MEDICAL COMPLICATIONS RESULTING FROM LONG-TERM EATING DISORDERS

For those who have been in their eating disorder for long periods of time, the compacting medical complications can have long-term—and even lethal—outcomes. One's body's immunity and ability to fight off disease suffer, and the person becomes weaker and unable to rebound in the same way as someone in a well-nourished, energized, and healthy body normally can.

One of the most concerning complications includes refeeding syndrome. The potential for this to happen is highest in those who are extremely malnourished from not eating and then begin to eat again either on their own or in a medical or treatment-type setting. One of the main goals of recovery is to reach a healthier weight by restoration, especially for those suffering from anorexia. The way restoration is facilitated by professionals is key to preventing refeeding syndrome. Refeeding syndrome happens when the intake of food causes a change in fluids and electrolytes that cause the body to work harder than it is capable of doing at that time, specifically having a dangerous impact on potassium and phosphorus levels. It can lead to all types of serious cardiac, respiratory, neurological, gastrointestinal, and other issues. For these reasons, thorough and consistent medical attention, as well as knowledge and awareness from the family and support system regarding the risks involved with refeeding, are vital. Throughout the process of refeeding, close observation of daily labs, vitals, cardiac functioning, as well as fluid and electrolyte replacement, all help to provide information on the body's response to receiving nourishment, how much it is capable of tolerating each step of the way, and what modifications need to be made to keep the person safe. Additionally, it is important to confirm that the doctor directing this process specializes in the medical complications of treating an eating disorder and is aware of the critical risks surrounding the refeeding process.

Hypoglycemia, which signifies low blood glucose levels resulting from restriction, is also extremely concerning because of the deadly outcomes that may arise when one's body does not have the required amounts of glucose to function. Another result of repetitive and enduring ED behaviors is organ failure. This can lead to cardiac arrest, coma, or brain dysfunction—all extremely serious conditions that bring one closer to death. Kidney failure is also common in those who have engaged in long periods of purging and laxative abuse because of accompanying dangerous levels of dehydration and low potassium levels, also referred to as hypokalemia. Finally, there are significant concerns for those with a chronic eating disorder who are still engaging in exercise. Prolonged activity with a refusal to supplement with the needed nutrition or energy intake further intensifies an overall energy shortage in the brain and body. This only contributes to further escalation of other medical difficulties already occurring in a weakened system.

Another complication resulting from the chronicity of an eating disorder, specifically anorexia, is the increased risk of osteopenia. Osteopenia signifies low bone density and strength; however, this condition is not always permanent and can be corrected with proper nutrition if caught early enough. While osteopenia can be asymptomatic, over time, it can lead to osteoporosis, which is permanent bone weakness that increases one's chance for fractures and breaks. Both conditions are caused by lower sex hormones resulting from restriction and a lack of vitamins and minerals needed to maintain strong bones.

MORTALITY RATES

As discussed in earlier chapters, the risk of death is higher for all types of ED presentations, with anorexia having been shown to be the most lethal mental health disorder. However, other types of eating disorders also pose a significant risk of death. This is due to not just the impact of the behaviors themselves but also factors such as the comorbidity of substance use and suicidality.

Specific mortality rates vary among studies and can be complicated by the crossover of specific behaviors; however, NEDA confirms a 10 percent mortality rate for anorexia. Rough estimates also show a mortality rate of 3.9 percent for bulimia and 5.2 percent for OSFED. OSFED was previously EDNOS, which included binge eating disorder presentations. Additionally, some studies have found higher mortality rates for men with eating disorders compared to women sufferers. Studies have also demonstrated an increased chance of death by natural causes, such as cancer, when equated with the general overall population.

Suicide Risk

There is a strong link between suicidal thoughts or ideation and eating disorders. The experience of feeling burdensome to others, worthless, hopeless, physically and mentally fatigued, or of carrying a "what's the point?" mentality, are only a few examples of experiences that contribute to the feeling of wanting to give up on life. Compounding these uncomfortable and scary feelings, the ED behaviors themselves trigger an inability to think clearly or rationally when in such a state. There are higher suicide attempts and incidents of death by suicide for those struggling with an eating disorder. The highest rates have been connected to bulimia. Alarmingly, Arcelus et al. (2011) found that one in five individuals who had an eating disorder died because of suicide. Some have found suicide as the principal cause of death for those suffering from an eating disorder. This occurrence is frequently linked to the high rate of depressive symptoms that also accompany this psychiatric illness.

One of the largest studies to date that looks at eating disorders and suicide was led by Shuyang Yao and followed individuals for six years in Sweden. Findings revealed that while there is a connection to comorbid disorders, such as depression or substance use, the increased risk of suicide is not completely due to additional psychiatric diagnoses or traits. This implies strong encouragement for future research and investigation into the link between the two.

Awareness for the warning signs of suicide is important. Depression is the most common disorder linked to suicide, but anxiety, substance use, and eating disorders can also intensify suicidal thoughts or actions. Whenever there is a noticeable shift in one's behavior, routine, or mood, it is important to pay attention. A particular event can instigate this change, such as a tragic loss, but this is not always the case. Understanding and being aware of risk factors as well as actions to take if you are concerned are ways to participate in preventing suicide. Making threats or talking about specific plans is one indicator someone may be considering suicide; so are signs of isolation and withdrawal from social groups and events. Alcohol and drug use is another sign due to the link between substance use and suicide. Rage, reckless behaviors, uncontrollable anger, and mood shifts are also signals to be sensitive to. Finally, previous suicide attempts and family history are risk factors. Risk factors are indicators or characteristics that increase the chance for someone being at a higher risk.

Just as crucial as it is to notice these signs, knowing what to do with the information in order to help someone when suspecting suicide is critical. It is imperative to voice your concerns if you are worried, while encouraging the individual to reach out for help. While it may feel uncomfortable or scary to speak up, letting potential suicide victims know you care and reminding them that they are not alone is helpful. Listening, offering hope, and just being present for someone are a few ways of supporting someone struggling with suicidal thoughts. Crisis lines, local mental health and crisis centers, hospitals, and local mental health providers are all available community resources to utilize as well.

Paralleling the importance of recognizing these concerning signs of possible suicide, knowing how to help support someone who is struggling with an eating disorder is critical. The next chapter will go into depth not only on best practices for providing accountability and support but also on what type of supportive resources are available to friends and family members of those who are suffering from an eating disorder.

7

Effects on Family and Friends

All types of eating disorders have the power and strength to significantly impact relationships. This illness does not discriminate between specific types of relationships either. Romantic, professional, plutonic, collegial, and familial relationships can all be influenced and changed in many ways. The shifts can occur during all phases of the disorder, starting with the initial signs and development in the beginning and lasting all the way through recovery. On the bright side, there are an abundance of support and useful outlets intended for those helping someone who is struggling with an eating disorder. Additionally, specific recommendations have been made as a result of research and case studies focused on the importance of maintaining interpersonal boundaries with an individual who has an eating disorder. This chapter will first look more closely at how this illness affects all types of relationships. Next, the focus will shift to the available support and resources for those in a position to help someone with an eating disorder before, during, and after treatment. Finally, time will be spent outlining the importance of self-care so that individuals with an eating disorder remain mindful of their own physical and mental well-being throughout the recovery journey.

IMPACT ON RELATIONSHIPS DURING THE EATING DISORDER

Ideally, the threat of relationships changing or disappearing could help incentivize individuals with eating disorders to move away from their illness. However, eating disorders often unfortunately replace meaningful and healthy relationships. Again, this is true for all types of relationships. The disappearance of strong relationships is influenced by the unhealthy relationship that develops between the person and the eating disorder. This becomes the focus of connection because it feels safe and grounding even though it grows to become destructive and unpredictable. Similar contributors to an eating disorder, such as insecurities, low self-esteem, and shame, can also sway those struggling to distance themselves from people altogether, especially those who they are close to. For example, shame or embarrassment caused by talking about or displaying ED behaviors of some concern may lead to avoidance of being around others or partaking in group activities or events. This starts a trend of isolation that only becomes more challenging to move away from and also leads to relationship strain, stress, and confusion.

Balancing time spent in both a relationship with one's eating disorder and in interpersonal relationships becomes demanding. An eating disorder works hard to maintain control and power with behaviors, which significantly impacts time spent with others and the desire to be around others when struggling. Often, the outcome is less time spent engaged with those who can support and provide accountability for recovery. As discussed in earlier chapters, eating disorders thrive on secrecy. While the intention can be to keep the behaviors hidden in order to prevent others from worrying or feeling scared, it is often interpreted differently. Consequently, family members, friends, and support people are kept confused and out of the loop, which can decrease the authenticity and closeness that relationships flourish upon.

Guilt, shame, and the feeling of being stuck are a few examples of feelings that cause persons with an eating disorder to create emotional space in a relationship. The assumption of being a burden or requiring too much support can lead to seclusion and fewer attempts at involving others in their struggles or attempts at recovery. Those in a supportive role can also easily become the target of negative emotional states, such as anger, frustration, and irritability.

Decreased physical intimacy is also common the further one becomes intertwined in an eating disorder. Body image concerns and insecurities about physical appearance often lead to desiring less physical touch, closeness, and sexual intimacy, which inevitably influences emotional connection.

HOW TO SUPPORT YOUR FRIEND OR FAMILY MEMBER BEFORE, DURING, AND AFTER TREATMENT

It is useful to keep in mind that you are not responsible for finding a solution for someone in the trenches of an eating disorder; instead, you are urged to be supportive and show empathy and compassion. This can be tricky because of the assumption that if one would just eat the food "normally," the eating disorder would resolve. This myth masks the reality that eating disorders develop and progress because of much more complicated and deeply rooted factors.

Understandably, relationship tension and detachment occur among friends, family members, and/or colleagues as one struggles with an eating disorder. This can easily make the person offering support in the role of a caretaker feel helpless. Those who are struggling are frequently unsure of what they need from others, which can also send mixed messages. Vague messages and communication make the journey even more confusing for those attempting to provide support. It is not uncommon to feel replaced as this illness becomes an outlet for someone to cope with a variety of feelings and/or emotional states. The illness begins to occupy more of the individual's time and energy every day, pushing further away those who are closest.

Many challenges will arise for all involved throughout the duration of an eating disorder. Initially, it can be very difficult to acknowledge that there is a problem and express concern for someone's behaviors. It is equally as hard to see someone changing emotionally and, at times, physically. Often, not only is the person with the eating disorder in denial but also those in the support role. It is important to remember that the sooner one finds help, the lower the chances are for a relapse. The culmination of events leading to an intervention, or strongly expressed encouragement to seek help, varies from person to person, but the initial leap into helping one find support is difficult for everyone. Fear for the relationship changing may postpone being more firm and assertive with expressed worry.

Once an individual is in treatment, others' fears and worry do not always subside. The high relapse rate for an eating disorder, coupled with the difficulty posed by interrupting behaviors, keeps caregivers, family, and friends afraid of regression. However, the added element of a treatment team or therapist can provide some ease by letting support people know they are no longer alone. Most treatment settings offer family therapy. This is in addition to other groups and experiences intended to help family and friends better understand the trajectory of an eating disorder, the steps in recovery, and potential responsibilities for those in a caregiver role. Psychoeducation, role-playing, and open process groups are only a few examples of activities and practices meant to provide support to those in this role. As the caregiver, you would be strongly encouraged to participate in any of these opportunities that are part of the individual's treatment, as well as support groups offered outside of it, in order to maintain an appropriate amount of connection to the recovery process. A family therapist is typically the point of contact for family and friends while one is in treatment or seeking help. They will guide, help set boundaries, provide feedback, and update family members or a group of friends on the status and progress of treatment. Unless the person is under 18 years of age, this is, of course, with permission.

Asking the individual how you can help takes the pressure away from feeling as though you should have the right answer or intervention. Let the individual know that concrete ideas, as well as what not to say or do, are useful in supporting them effectively. For example, using food talk or specifics about their behaviors is often activating and a potential precipitant of frustration or upset. This is a difficult realm to navigate, so conversations that help iron out specifics with regard to language and topic areas of conversation are imperative.

Often, individuals may not know what they need, so it is essential to make them aware that you are there to support them when they are ready. Along these lines, the journey of supporting someone may entail trial and error. Therefore, it is important to learn from scenarios that do not go ideally or as planned while also not blaming yourself. You are navigating just as much new territory as the individual working toward recovery is. This gradual process can be overwhelming, scary, and exhausting for everyone.

Setting Boundaries

In order to support someone else, it is important to also take care of yourself. One thing this may entail is setting boundaries and limits that feel uncomfortable but are also what the suffering person requires at that time in order to get better. Boundaries and limits come in many forms depending on each individual's situation and needs but may involve putting parameters around the content of conversation and language, time spent with specific people and/or in certain places, and the like. Setting boundaries has many purposes, but one of the most significant is helping one not revert to old patterns and habits. Changing things up interpersonally or intrapersonally offers the opportunity to try something different when previous dynamics within a support system are no longer working. Often this can be practiced and implemented in a higher level of care setting before it is more independently applied in an outpatient setting where the individual has more autonomy.

Resistance and regression are common throughout the trajectory of an ED treatment. It is during these difficult moments, or even longer periods of times, that encouragement from family and friends to try something different is so imperative. This can be conveyed in the form of setting boundaries. If the persons struggling feels that you are colluding with the illness, it is much easier to resort to behaviors that are comfortable and provide momentary relief. On the other hand, if they experience you fighting against their eating disorder and encouraging change, they may be more willing to try different forms of coping, knowing they have support in doing so. This strategy may feel less isolating for persons with an eating disorder.

Setting limits or boundaries also lessens the potential for enabling to occur. Enabling means providing someone with the resources needed to do something. In the case of an eating disorder, this can happen when a friend or family member's attempt to fix the problem for the person struggling actually further contributes to keeping the person in the illness. Enabling tendencies or actions may take a while for anyone to notice because they are masked by the perception of help. The person struggling with an eating disorder may also interpret this as useful or supportive. It can be a challenge to view enabling patterns as more detrimental than helpful because pulling back in order to maintain boundaries feels uncomfortable or hurtful. A treatment team member, family therapist, and outpatient provider are all examples of those who may notice and intervene. When they point out the destructive scenario happening, especially if it is occurring while the individual is in treatment, they can help steer family or friends in a more useful direction. Practice toward not engaging in enabling habits while someone is in treatment can help prepare for the transition out, where there is less supervision and support. The hope is that time and space dedicated to learning how to help individuals while in treatment or receiving more support will prepare them for a step-down to less accountability.

While the space after treatment offers more autonomy, choice, and independence, no one is expected to engage in recovery alone. One way to help persons with an eating disorder is to encourage and advocate for them to follow the recommendations of the team or clinicians involved in their care. This is not to be confused with doing the work for the person; instead, it is taking part appropriately, by reinforcing what the professionals have strongly suggested. For example, reminding one to employ self-care activities, such as practicing adequate sleep habits and relaxation exercises or engaging in daily hygiene, can be a significant form of help from a family member or friend. This also means following and implementing guidelines and boundaries set by the treatment team for those in the helping or support role.

It is important to keep in mind that practice around setting boundaries may illuminate awareness of some relationships that are no longer helpful or conducive, especially when it comes to the challenging task of sustaining recovery. This realization can occur for either side of the relationship— the individual with the eating disorder or those attempting to support and provide accountability.

Maintaining Boundaries

Maintaining set boundaries is crucial when it comes to helping individuals progress in their recovery, especially because boundaries can serve as a form of security. Because relationship stress can also exacerbate or lead to behaviors, it is important to make sure the relationship is a supportive outlet in one's recovery rather than one that makes space for enabling, colluding, or fixing. On the flip side, Tom and colleagues' research (2005) points out that a healthy and stable relationship can actually serve as a protective factor for eating disorders, meaning that it can potentially serve as security from further engagement in the illness. This is partly due to the safety of a partnership diminishing the harmful impact that body image distortions can have on sustaining the illness. Consistent check-ins, both internally and with the person struggling, about set limits and boundary crossings can be difficult; however, this is essential to upholding the necessary structure, support, and amount of contact for recovery. Maintaining boundaries is also a great form of self-care for all involved to practice and implement into daily life and relationships.

How to Talk to Someone with an Eating Disorder

Knowing what to say or how to talk to persons suffering from an eating disorder is important. Those struggling feel anxious and overwhelmed and as if a spotlight is focused on them. Therefore, it is beneficial for interactions and conversations to center around recent interests, family events, exciting news or occasions, as well as past experiences with that person. Questions or comments involving food, appearance, weight, meal plans, and so forth can easily become a source of distress that can lead to regression and distance.

It is so important to seek out education and knowledge on your own. Do not be afraid to ask questions and demand answers about this complicated illness that is not well known to many. This may be from the person you are supporting and that person's treatment team or even from ED specialists in your area.

HOW TO TAKE CARE OF YOURSELF

Being in a relationship with someone with an eating disorder is not only scary but also exhausting and draining. It is important to develop a consistent and strong self-care routine in order to maintain adequate sleep, nutritional needs, space alone, and emotional stability during an incredibly challenging period. This may involve planned time with others, as well as alone time to reset and reenergize. It is important to be aware of how this caretaking or support role can impact other relationships. Constant worry, uncertainty, and focus surrounding the person who is sick not only lessens the attention and concern for those wanting to give care and support but also minimizes *their* well-being. In order to fully support someone else, you must also be looking out for your own needs. Limiting time spent with the individual struggling may provide the structure necessary to ensure adequate time to engage in self-care and plan for useful space away. Communicating an intention to stick to these needs in order to maintain accountability is helpful. This also provides a role model for the difficult balance of self-care and taking care of others. One very helpful outlet and form of self-care is engaging in your own therapy. It provides a needed space for processing out loud and with someone removed from the situation and in a neutral position.

The idea of having to monitor this balance on your own is understandably scary. The good news is that there are many organizations, groups, and resources designed and implemented to be of support to those in the position of helping or caring for someone struggling with or working toward recovery from an eating disorder.

NEDA, MEDA (Multi-Service Eating Disorders Association), Eating Disorder Hope, and state-specific ED foundations are all examples of online resources that have extensive material, research, and updated knowledge available. Organizations such as these also initiate planned events, regional conferences, walks, meetings, and fundraisers with the goal of raising awareness about eating disorders and providing a place for all to convene for this cause. These are highly recommended resources to utilize when learning more about this illness and building a support network. NEDA has also designed and made available specific, in-depth toolkits for parents, friends, educators, coaches, and others in similar roles. These resources are free and provide a range of information about eating disorders, including basic knowledge, insurance help, treatment options, and insight around supporting someone who may be or is struggling.

It is important to be aware of how this serious illness can affect many spheres of life, especially interpersonal connections and relationships. Relationships extend into and influence other realms of life, too, such as work, school, or socialization. However, as described, there is existing support for everyone involved, including those in a support or familial role. It is strongly encouraged to wade through this journey with others and the available resources, because doing it alone is not easy. It also takes time and patience to learn how to engage in self-care, boundaries, and the offering of appropriate support for one struggling order to minimize the negative effects on family and friends. The next chapter will go further into the prevention of eating disorders, as well as look at support on a broader scale.

8

Prevention

There are several ways that we think we can prevent eating disorders: education, support, and destigmatization. First, preventing eating disorders might be as simple as providing information to the world about eating disorders. This chapter starts by exploring what education currently exists around eating disorders and what institutions and/or organizations are contributing to ED prevention. While support through treatment for eating disorders has already been addressed, there is other support to prevent eating disorders. How these other supports can prevent eating disorders will be identified and investigated. Finally, the chapter will address how destigmatizing eating disorders and other mental health disorders can also lead to the prevention of eating disorders and, specifically, how to destigmatize eating disorders and other mental health disorders.

EDUCATION

The main source of education for individuals in the United States is formalized primary or secondary education (e.g., public or private school). Unfortunately, a study by the National Center for Biotechnology Information indicated that less than 30 percent of first-year college students had been exposed to ED programming during primary or secondary education and virtually no first-year students had been exposed to ED prevention during primary or secondary education. After primary or secondary

education, individuals have historically turned to websites, books, or peri-
odicals (e.g., newspapers and magazines) for education—although health
education websites and social media and social networking sites are
quickly catching up as platforms to educate the masses. There are hundreds of organizations that work to educate, but the following organizations are the biggest and best at providing education around eating
disorders.

The National Association of Anorexia Nervosa and Associated Disorders (ANAD) is "a non-profit organization working in the areas of support,
awareness, advocacy, referral, education, and prevention." ANAD was the
first organization created to address ED education in the United States,
and it provides resources about eating disorders to individuals who struggle, as well as to their families, friends, schools, and communities. The
organization was founded by Vivian Hanson Meehan in the early 1970s
when she was unable to locate any ED resources for a family member who
had recently been diagnosed with anorexia. As a nurse, she reached out to
experts in the medical field and was warned that anorexia was too rare to
be studied sufficiently. According to Meehan herself, she hoped to prove
these experts wrong by placing a classified ad in a local newspaper looking
for others who were searching for information about eating disorders.
Within days, Vivian had eight replies to her local ad before the advertisement was distributed to a national audience that supplied thousands of
phone calls and letters. In response to this need for resources, Vivian
launched the first helpline and referral service for anorexia and associated
eating disorders in the nation. She also created a support group in her
home, and eventually support groups popped up across the country. These
groups continue to provide complimentary peer-to-peer support and self-
help for the individuals and families affected by eating disorders. While it
is presumably the oldest resource for eating disorders, ANAD continues to
be one of the best resources.

The Multi-Service Eating Disorder Association (MEDA) was founded in
1994 by Rebecca Manley, who had struggled with disordered eating since
the third grade. She helped grow the New England nonprofit that started
in her basement in Boston into a professional organization that touches
tens of thousands impacted by eating disorders annually. MEDA has a
vision of "a community without eating disorders that promotes a positive
body culture." "Educating the public eating disorders and body image" is
one of the ways that MEDA is touching so many thousands, through its
education and awareness initiative, "The Sooner the Better." The Sooner
the Better is aimed at educating communities on body confidence as well
as signs and symptoms of disordered eating and eating disorders. In addition, MEDA offers educational workshops on these topics and others.
MEDA also hosts an annual conference that assembles more than

275 eating disorders professionals together to discuss the latest in research and therapies.

Mirror Mirror is a website originally created in 1997 by Colleen Thompson while she was recovering from an eating disorder. Her mission was "to provide education and support for others with eating disorders while also educating herself and working through some of the issues that she struggled with personally." Today, the mission of the organization is to build upon Thompson's work "by providing information, education, and support to the community, including people dealing with eating disorders themselves and loved ones that want to support friends or family members with eating disorders." Mirror Mirror aims to help individuals recovering from eating disorders, but it also aims "to help parents, educators, and other adults that work with children and adolescents to be more aware of the signs and symptoms of eating disorders, so they can provide early intervention when needed." While the organization is focused on educating to prevent eating disorders, it is also quick to highlight that eating disorders are often unavoidable and that support and other resources will be provided to individuals and their families if an eating disorder develops.

Eating Disorder Hope is another organization that offers education. The mission of this organization is "to foster an appreciation of one's uniqueness and value in the world, unrelated to appearance, achievement or applause," and it "promotes ending eating disordered behavior, embracing life and pursuing recovery from eating disorders." Its resources include newsletters, articles, interviews, and presentations on eating disorders as well as information on support groups and recovery tools.

The National Eating Disorder Association, NEDA, is the largest nonprofit organization devoted to supporting individuals and families affected by eating disorders. Its mission is "to serve as a catalyst for prevention, cures, and access to quality care." NEDA has educational tools with basic information about eating disorders as well as screening tools. It also provides education about how to support family members and friends who might be struggling with an eating disorder as well as education for various professionals who might encounter eating disorders, including teachers, coaches, doctors, and dentists. The organization has a blog and regularly posts recent articles and information about eating disorders.

While the Eating Disorder Foundation (EDF) is a nonprofit organization "devoted to helping people with eating disorders, their families and their friends to rebuild shattered lives," it also "works to increase awareness about disorders that can ruin and even end lives . . . [with] a two-pronged approach center[ed] on a wide-range of free support services and on extensive educational efforts provided at no charge to schools and community groups." EDF has a vision of preventing and eliminating eating disorders with a mission of serving as "an effective resource in the prevention and elimination of eating disorders through education, support, and advocacy." It engages in education through "initiatives together with timely support and helps in identifying appropriate treatment options for individuals with eating disorders and their families."

The Foundation for Research and Education in Eating Disorders (FREED) is a nonprofit organization that was created in 2012 "to help lead the fight against eating disorders." The mission of FREED is "to help determine the causes and risks associated with developing eating disorders; facilitate the development of treatments; and promote education, prevention and recovery from these illnesses." The vision of the organization is "a nation in which eating disorders are fully preventable, manageable and recoverable." As a nonprofit serving Americans impacted by eating disorders, FREED relies on volunteers and donations to accomplish its mission.

The Eating Disorders Coalition (EDC) advances "the recognition of eating disorders as a public health priority throughout the United States." With a focus on educating the legislature, EDC works to change policy around eating disorders. Its specific goals are to "raise awareness among policy makers and the public at large about the serious health risks posed by eating disorders, promote federal support for improved access to care, increase resources for education, prevention, and improved training, increase funding and support for scientific research on the etiology, prevention, and treatment of eating disorders, promote initiatives that support the healthy development of children, and mobilize concerned citizens to advocate on behalf of people with eating disorders, their families, and professionals in the field."

Founded in 1993, the Academy for Eating Disorders (AED) is "a global professional association committed to leadership in eating disorders research, education, treatment, and prevention." AED works to educate the public on eating disorders and their treatment. It also works to keep helping professionals connected and collaborating with each other on recent developments in ED research. One of the primary AED educational events is the annual International Conference on Eating Disorders (ICED), a conference that includes information on eating disorders, from basic science to cutting-edge research in the field.

Established in 1985, the International Association of Eating Disorders Professionals (iaedp) is a global organization recognized for providing education and training to medical providers and helping professionals treating eating disorders. The iaedp publishes *The Eating Disorders Review*, an online professional journal addressing contemporary ED treatment, and also hosts an annual symposium that gathers medical providers and helping professionals to educate and collaborate on innovative information related to the treatment of eating disorders. It also prepares medical providers and helping professionals to treat eating disorders through a highly respected eating disorder certificate. The certification confirms academic coursework as well as supervised field work with eating disorders and culminates with a written examination.

The National Alliance on Mental Illness (NAMI), the National Institute of Mental Health (NIMH), and the World Health Organization (WHO) are also organizations that provide education on eating disorders— although their scope is broader and geared toward general mental health and wellness. Created by a small group of families in 1979, NAMI is the country's largest grassroots mental health organization devoted to Americans impacted by mental health and is the nation's leading voice on mental health. According to NAMI, the association has more than 500 local affiliates who work in communities "to raise awareness and provide support and education that was not previously available to those in need." While the education programs change periodically, there are programs about mental health for youth and their parents as well as other family members. There are also mental health programs for adults with specialty programming for military service members and veterans as well as their families and caregivers. NAMI also provides extensive education programming for mental health professionals. In addition to individual education, NAMI is also involved in educating communities through public awareness events and activities as well as public policy and legislation.

NIMH is the principal government agency in the United States for research on mental health. NIMH is one of the 27 institutes and centers that make up the National Institutes of Health (NIH), the largest biomedical research agency in the world. The vision of NIMH is "a world in which mental illnesses are prevented and cured" and its goal is "to transform the understanding and treatment of mental illnesses through basic and clinical research, paving the way for prevention, recovery, and cure."

WHO works worldwide "to promote health, keep the world safe, and serve the vulnerable." The goal of the organization is "to ensure that a billion more people have universal health coverage, to protect a billion more people from health emergencies, and provide a further billion people with better health and well-being." One of the primary goals of the organization is mental health education. WHO began on April 7, 1948, and this date is celebrated as World Health Day. The organization, headquartered in Geneva, Switzerland, currently employs more than 7,000 individuals in 150 offices in countries across the world.

The American Psychological Association (APA) is "the leading scientific and professional organization representing psychology in the United States, with more than 118,000 researchers, educators, clinicians, consultants and students as its members." The mission of the APA is "to promote the advancement, communication, and application of psychological science and knowledge to benefit society and improve lives by:

- utilizing psychology to make a positive impact on critical societal issues.
- elevating the public's understanding of, regard for, and use of psychology.
- preparing the discipline and profession of psychology for the future.
- strengthening APA's standing as an authoritative voice for psychology."

The American Psychiatric Association (also APA) is an organization of more than 3,500 psychiatrists in practice, research, and academia working together to ensure compassionate and effective treatment for individuals struggling with mental health. Its vision is "a society that has available, accessible quality psychiatric diagnosis and treatment." The mission of this APA is "to:

- promote the highest quality care for individuals with mental illness, including substance use disorders, and their families.
- promote psychiatric education and research.
- advance and represent the profession of psychiatry.
- serve the professional needs of its membership."

The goal of the organization is "to promote the rights and best interests of patients and those actually or potentially making use of psychiatric services for mental illness."

While all of these organizations are working tirelessly to educate the United States and the world on eating disorders, there is clearly a long way to go and much work to be done to prevent eating disorders.

SUPPORT

Again, treatment has already been examined, but what support is available to prevent eating disorders? First, there is tremendous support available through some of the organizations already mentioned in this chapter. In addition to education, ANAD provides support groups across the country and a professional helpline. It also has specialized support programming called the Grocery Buddy (which provides support for those who might struggle in a grocery store due to their eating disorder) and recovery mentors (who help individuals struggling with an eating disorder or disordered eating with their recovery). MEDA as well as NEDA have numerous support tools, including forums and live chats as well as an ED helpline during regular business hours. NEDA also provides resources around support groups, including what types are available and where they are located.

These support groups can be open or closed and they can be run by professionals or by members of the ED recovery community. Eating Disorder Hope also provides resources for locating support groups. Mirror Mirror has a support group structure and allows individuals in communities across the country to utilize its goals and rules to form ED groups. There are also Ten Steps for ED recovery and guidelines for the road to recovery. EDF has comparable resources, but it also offers support groups from its headquarters in Denver, Colorado. There are various support groups for individuals struggling with eating disorders as well as separate support groups for their family and friends. EDF also offers support groups for specialized populations, including men, the gay and lesbian community, and athletes, in Denver as well as virtual support groups accessible nationwide.

The organizations that provide education as well as support have been mentioned, but there are also ED and other mental health organizations focused more on support than on education. Eating Disorders Anonymous (EDA) is a fellowship of individuals who support each other through sharing experiences with treatment and recovery. The only requirement for membership is a desire to recover from an eating disorder. It is very similar to the better-known Alcoholics Anonymous. In EDA, individuals in the organization help each other identify and celebrate milestones of recovery as well as encourage a focus on the solution, not the problem. According to EDA, "solutions have to do with recognizing life choices and making them responsibly" and "diets and weight management techniques do not solve our thinking problems." The motto for EDA is "balance—not abstinence."

Overeaters Anonymous (OA) is a comparable program and is a fellowship of individuals who are recovering from compulsive overeating. The organization welcomes anyone who wants to interrupt compulsive eating, and the primary purpose is "to abstain from compulsive eating and compulsive food behaviors and to carry the message of recovery through the Twelve Steps of OA to those who still suffer." The organization suggests that symptoms might look different from person to person but the common denominator is a powerlessness over food and a life that has become unmanageable as a result.

While these organizations provide these support resources and groups, treatment centers across the United States as well as university counseling centers provide these support resources and groups too.

DESTIGMATIZATION

How can eating disorders be destigmatized? First, mental health needs to be destigmatized. Presumably, the more than we talk about eating disorders and other mental health issues, the less stigmatized and the more preventable they will become. NAMI is one of many organizations looking to destigmatize mental health. NAMI claims that society has stereotyped views about mental illness and how it affects people. For example, there is a notion that individuals with mental illnesses are violent and dangerous. The truth is that these individuals are actually more at risk of being violently attacked or harming themselves, not other people. NAMI also suggests that "many people with serious mental illness are challenged doubly. On one hand, they struggle with the symptoms and disabilities that result from the disease. On the other, they are challenged by the stereotypes and prejudice that result from misconceptions about mental illness." As a result of both, individuals with mental health issues are often deprived of a quality of life that should include a decent job, safe housing, and suitable health care. We are still learning about the actual impact of mental health as we are only beginning to destigmatize it. More research needs to be completed to effectively explain the depth of prejudice against mental health.

Eating disorders can also be destigmatized by widening the lens of beauty and changing the way that society evaluates a body. There are hundreds of movements around beauty ideals and body image including the Body Positivity Movement, the Body Image Movement, Love Your Body, and No Body Shame. These social movements are rooted in the belief that all human beings should have a positive body image and love their bodies while challenging the ways in which society presents and views the physical body.

Many organizations are also getting involved in awareness activities around eating disorders. Notably, Eating Disorder Awareness Week is an annual campaign that aims to raise awareness about eating disorders as well as provide resources for those who might be interested in treatment. The 2019 theme for Eating Disorder Awareness Week was "Let's Get Real" and the goal was "to expand the conversation and share stories that are not often heard in the media; stories about the reality of eating disorders and personal experiences centered on treatment." During this week, there are typically hundreds of events hosted across the country, including informational sessions for the legislature, ED awareness walks, body image workshops, and educational events hosted by community centers and secondary schools and universities. Additionally, NEDA promotes a social media campaign where individuals ask questions, share stories, and learn about eating disorders from other individuals.

On a regular basis, NEDA also hosts NEDA Walks, and there are approximately 100 cities with tens of thousands of participants of all ages and backgrounds. NEDA Walks are the largest ED awareness events in the country and aim to be "inspirational, community-building events where passionate walkers raise money to fund eating disorders education, prevention, and support, as well as advocacy and research initiatives." These walks include activities that promote body positivity, motivational guest speakers, and the walk itself to represent unity in the battle against eating disorders.

As previously mentioned, NAMI is on the forefront of destigmatizing mental illness and has grounded its destigmatization campaign on the following platform:

> Most people who live with mental illness have, at some point, been blamed for their condition. They've been called names. Their symptoms have been referred to as a phase or something they can control if they tried. They have also been discriminated against without consequence. Stigma causes people to feel ashamed for something that is beyond of their control. Worst of all, stigma prevents people from seeking the help they need. For a group of people who already carry such a heavy burden, stigma is an unacceptable addition to their pain. And while stigma has reduced in recent years, the pace of progress has not been quick enough.

NAMI identified nine ways to fight stigma:

1. Talk openly about mental health (as mentioned earlier in this chapter).
2. Educate yourself and others about mental health (also as mentioned in this chapter).
3. Be conscious of language—especially with regard to using mental health terms as descriptors—for example, "She's eating like an anorexic" or "That's so borderline."
4. Provide equality to both physical and mental health.
5. Showing compassion for those with mental illness.
6. Empowering those with mental illness as opposed to shaming them.
7. Be honest about treatment needs to yourself and to others.
8. Challenge the media about furthering stigma.
9. Don't harbor self-stigma.

These are just a few small steps that one of the leading organizations on mental health advocated for; there are so many more ways that we can destigmatize eating disorders and mental health!

In order to prevent eating disorders, we need to educate, support, and destigmatize. This chapter has covered what education is out there and who is contributing to ED prevention through education. It also covered the preventive support that exists outside of treatment. Finally, this chapter covered how destigmatizing eating disorders and other mental health disorders can also lead to the prevention of eating disorders and, specifically, how to destigmatize eating disorders and other mental health disorders. Hopefully with more education, support, and destigmatization, eating disorders can be prevented.

9

Issues and Controversies

There are a number of issues and controversies that surround the topic of eating disorders. These include, but are not limited to, societal influences on eating disorders, social media and eating disorders, incorporating exercise into ED treatment, and insurance coverage for eating disorders. This list is not comprehensive, but it highlights the greatest issues creating the biggest controversies.

SOCIETAL INFLUENCES

As discussed in chapter 3, evidence shows that sociocultural or societal influences play an enormous role in the development of eating disorders. As has been mentioned, the most predominant images in our culture today suggest that beauty is equated with thinness for women and a lean, muscular body for men. As this book has also already suggested, individuals with these beauty ideals have a greater risk of developing body dissatisfaction, which can lead to ED behaviors. The increased obsession of the media with the perfect body may contribute to unrealistic body ideals in individuals with and without eating disorders. An increase in access to global media and technological advances such as photoshop and airbrushing in addition to plastic surgery have also further skewed our perception of attainable beauty standards. This section will help break down further the list created by the online American women's magazine, *Bustle*, including photoshop and airbrushing; the thin ideal; the diet culture; Fitspo challenges; the lack of racial and body type diversity on television; and typecasting plus-size actors.

Photoshop and Airbrushing

There have been heated debates about whether photoshop or airbrushing can be blamed for ED development. Back in 2011, the American Medical Association released a statement confirming the contribution of the practice of photoshopping models to eating disorders. Additionally, NEDA suggested that "numerous correlational and experimental studies have linked exposure to the thin ideal in mass media to body dissatisfaction, internalization of the thin ideal, and disordered eating among women. When our cultural norm is to photoshop or airbrush an already thin model to the degree that her head actually appears wider than her waist, it's not possible to contest that the idealization of size plays a role in eating disorder development."

The Thin Ideal

Society inundates men and women with images of perfect bodies as well as diet and exercise all of the time. From fashion advertisements to television shows to the pop-up advertisements on the internet, studies show that media do contribute to the development of eating disorders. In March 2015, the School of Public Health at Harvard University published its findings on the connection between advertising and ED development. Harvard targeted advertisement critic and author, Jean Kilbourne, known for her documentary, *Killing Us Softly*, which focuses on images of women in the media, pointed out that "most Americans are exposed to an average of 3,000 advertisements daily. Since the focus of most of these advertisements is a depiction of idealized beauty, the advertisements ultimately contribute to body dissatisfaction among women and girls." In its response to the topic, Harvard addressed the issue this way: "The American ideal of beauty has become so pervasive that 50% of three- to six-year-old girls worry about their weight. And on the island of Fiji, the arrival of television heralded a boom in dieting among women and girls who before then hadn't realized that there was something wrong with them."

Clearly the media has a significant influence on how we think we should look. Regardless of gender, men and women are striving to look like fashion models and movie stars.

Diet Culture

Diet commercials are constantly appearing on our television screens, in magazines, and on internet pop-up ads, telling us that losing weight will make us happy. Standing in line at the grocery store, there are magazines covering the checkout stand with the newest and best diets. Regularly, there is a new diet that will be the diet to end all diets—Atkins, Keto, Paleo, Mediterranean, and Weight Watchers, to name a few. Dieting has become an obsession in North America.

Billions of dollars are spent each year on diets. If diets really work, why are there so many of them? New diets regularly appear because old diets didn't work, and that is because, put simply, diets don't work. Period. Most of the diets on the market aren't even healthy. They often deprive individuals of the proper nutrition needed to survive.

The diet industry cannot take all of the blame for the societal obsession with the perfect body. It is unfortunate that society values what is on the outside more than what is on the inside. Until society can start loving and accepting each other for who we are and not what we look like, the diet culture will likely remain.

Fitspo Challenges

There always seems to be a new Fitspo challenge (i.e., a challenge to inspire people to get fit and healthy) trending on social media for men and women to try to meet. While these posts could be great motivators to start living a healthier lifestyle, recent research confirms that "fitspiration posts" are often just one more way society influences women to feel poorly about their bodies. In turn, this drop in self-esteem could be contributing to the development of eating disorders among women.

In a recent study conducted by Flinders University, "130 women were divided into two groups. One group was shown travel images while the other was shown a variety of fitspiration images. Unsurprisingly, the second group ended up reporting more negative moods and body dissatisfaction afterwards than the first."

Lack of Racial and Body Type Diversity on Television

Fortunately, Hollywood is becoming more inclusive of race as well as body types than it has in the past, but it is safe to say that women on television and in movies are still disproportionately white and thin. According to NEDA, whenever diversity isn't lacking in TV, women and girls of color are more likely to show satisfaction with their bodies: "Black-oriented television shows may serve a protective function; Hispanic and Black girls and women who watch more Black-oriented television have higher body satisfaction."

While there are so many reasons the diversity problem in Hollywood needs to be remedied now, the role it plays in influencing women and girls of color—and also just plus-size women in general—to develop eating disorders is definitely convincing.

Typecasting Plus-Size Actors

Similar to the increasing inclusivity of race as well as body type, Hollywood has been improving in how it casts plus-size women in roles. That said, plus-size actors have typically played the role of the sidekick to the tall and thin beautiful woman on television and in movies for years. It has only been recently that some plus-size actresses and models have enjoyed access to the kind of exposure that thin women have. Intentional or not, how plus-size women are represented in media is one more way society influences all women to adopt disordered eating habits to attain the thin ideal.

What can be done about societal influences? Because different forms of mass media (e.g., magazines, television, and the internet) are likely contributing to the development of eating disorders, efforts are being made to teach media literacy to children and adolescents as a prevention strategy. Children and adolescents are being taught that the body image ideal within our society is actually not achievable, through attempts to educate them on the process or photoshop and airbrushing. This education is often startling for children and adolescents.

Parents and other caregivers can also have a tremendous influence on how children and adolescents view themselves. It is important to reiterate that parents do not cause eating disorders in their children, but they cannot necessarily prevent them since eating disorders are biologically driven illnesses. However, parents and caregivers can work to build resilience and self-acceptance in their children and adolescents, encouraging them to be proud of who they are and to be less concerned about their size or shape. Parents and other caregivers can also teach their children the value of healthy eating. Informing children and adolescents that diets do not work and that eating three healthy meals and a few snacks a day with moderate exercise will allow their body to settle at its natural set point. It is also important to teach children and adolescents that no one food, as long as it is eaten in moderation, can make them fat. Finally, parents and other caregivers can be good role models by no longer purchasing fashion magazines and diet products and by focusing on learning to love and accept their size and shape while encouraging children and adolescents to do the same.

To help address unhealthy body images in the media, the British Broadcasting Corporation (BBC) reported that countries such as France are setting the standards for a healthy body weight for all models in the fashion industry. France was able to take the lead in this industry by requiring a certificate from a qualified medical provider attesting to the overall health of the model based on their body mass index (BMI) while taking into account their age, weight, and body type. The law also requires that photoshopped media must be labeled before they are distributed. Since the creation of the French law, other countries such as Israel, Italy, and Spain have developed laws around the health of models.

INFLUENCE OF SOCIAL MEDIA

According to the HuffPost, "social media has effectively made its way into every classroom, dinner table, and workplace. Whether it is used by children, teenagers, or adults, everyone seems to have a presence in the social media world. With a wide range of social media platforms used among all age groups including Instagram, Facebook, Snapchat, and Twitter, it can be increasingly difficult to escape the pressures and influences of social media." Unfortunately, social media can have a strong influence on food as well as how people feel about their body. Many individuals on social media are reporting their food choices and exercise regimens as well as highlighting their bodies for all to see. For individuals struggling with an eating disorder, being inundated with food and exercise as well as perfect bodies can create heightened levels of stress and anxiety.

Although social media itself is not the sole cause of an eating disorder, it has been confirmed to be connected to individuals to engaging in disordered patterns of eating. According to a research study from the Children's Hospital of Eastern Ontario, "social media is a causal risk factor for the development of eating disorders and has a strong influence on a person's body dissatisfaction, eating patterns, and poor self-concept. Individuals begin to constantly compare themselves to thin models and their peers as well as famous social media influencers and begin to feel inadequate about their own self-image." The research goes on to note that "it has been increasingly difficult to avoid the constant peer pressure surrounding the ideal body type. The presence of social media in everyday life is so large that individuals now care about the opinions of people that they have never met before. Body shamers use social media as a platform to talk negatively about someone's image and it strongly affects the emotional well-being of individuals who already struggle with their relationship with food. The social media platform has also made it easier for bullying to infiltrate an individual's daily life, beyond the parameters of the school day." According to NEDA, "as many as 65% of people with eating disorders say bullying contributed to their condition." The obsession over self-image and fitting in on social media has also opened the door for more bullying to occur. Bullying can have a tremendous influence on individuals' concept of self as well as their behavior. For example, individuals who have experienced bullying are more likely to binge eat or skip meals to manage emotions.

In 2014, a research team from the University of Pittsburgh School of Medicine asked 1,765 American adults between the ages of 19 and 32 to answer a series of questions that described their social media usage. Through this research, the research team was also evaluating risks related to developing ED symptoms. Their findings revealed that "the subjects who spent the most time engaged with social media each day had 2.2 times the risk of developing eating disorders. Additionally, those who most frequently checked their social media feeds weekly carried 2.6 times the risk."

Another social media risk is that individuals struggling with eating often measure their achievements and accomplishments against their peers and often feel as though they are inadequate or don't measure up. With a constant stream of casual acquaintances sharing news of their diplomas and promotions, new friends and boyfriends, and family outings and vacations or international adventures, self-hate and the ability to appreciate personal successes can fall away quickly. This can be even more devastating if an individual is missing out on life due to ED treatment or simply the eating disorder itself.

The growing number of social media outlets continue to make it more difficult to escape. Although it is important to note that some individuals on social media report feeling as though their feelings of inadequacy and worthlessness are multiplied and their isolation increased, it is important to point out that some individuals feel strongly that social media allows them a voice and to feel supported. Sometimes, social media can be of great comfort to individuals with eating disorders by providing a connection to others who understand and can relate to their struggles.

There are other ways that social media can be affirmative. Targeted criticism over the use of unrealistic model images in our everyday sources of media have been occurring with more frequency. Online social media campaigns and Twitter responses to body shaming and sexist comments are becoming more common. Recovery-oriented blogs and message boards can also be extremely valuable; ED awareness or support events can be publicized there. In these ways, it also becomes easier for individuals to stand up and lobby against injustices and challenge stigma around eating disorders. Social media can promote recovery and create a sense of community that can make someone struggling with an eating disorder feel less alone.

So what can we do to protect ourselves online and use the social media in a safe and beneficial way? According to Mirror Mirror,

> the most important rule is to be mindful and aware of the composed nature of social media. Try to view those perfect yet posed and edited Instagram selfies as what they are and limit your usage of certain websites when they feel overwhelming or all-consuming. Be mindful of the fact that the content you see is often a façade and that underlying fragilities are easily concealed

behind smoke and mirrors. You can block people or accounts, report inappropriate content, or tailor your feed on social media sites to filter particular users or groups. Ultimately, there is always the deactivate button and putting all social media on blackout, even for temporary periods, can be empowering. Recognize the warning signs, take back control of the mouse pad and press the shutdown key. Try to protect yourself as much as you can, and reach out for appropriate support when necessary.

Pro-Ana, Pro-Mia, and Thinspiration Sites

What are pro-ana or pro-mia, and why do they have websites or other social media outlets? And what is thinspiration? Pro-ana stands for pro-anorexia and pro-mia stands for pro-bulimia. There are pro-ana and pro-mia websites, blogs, chats, and forums, as well as Facebook, Instagram, Snapchat, Twitter, Pinterest, and Tumblr sites littered throughout cyberspace. In a nutshell, these websites or social media outlets support individuals with anorexia and/or bulimia. Both pro-ana and pro-mia sites often include thinspiration—photographs of very underweight individuals that are used for inspiration. The thinspiration (thinspo, for short) movement supports and encourages people to get ultrathin, in most cases below what would be considered as a healthy weight. In addition to thinspiration, the pro-ana and pro-mia sites often provide inspirational pictures of very thin individuals and accompanying stories that encourage an eating disorder. Medical professionals cite the "primary sources" for tips and tricks for extreme weight loss. As a means of offering support to each other, pictures are posted that show vast weight reduction, visible and protruding bone structure (collarbone, spine, ribs, leg bones, jawbones), and tips on hiding purging methods, hunger suppression tactics, and even ways to prevent vomit from eroding teeth. Interestingly, the owners of these types of sites usually have a disclaimer or warning statement on the home page that supports the idea that living with an eating disorder is a choice. One site, for example, states the following message: "This site does not encourage that you develop an eating disorder. This is a site for those who ALREADY have an eating disorder and do not wish to go into recovery. If you do not already have an eating disorder, better it is that you do not develop one now. You may wish to leave."

Another similar statement is this: "Heavy dietary changes and exercise can be a deadly hazard to your life. Nothing is more precious than your life. Please make sustainable changes only. It won't happen in a day. It will take its time. Consistency and perseverance will get you there."

As a rule, members of the pro-ana sites do not recruit people into the world of eating disorders. Rather, they provide individuals with existing eating disorders with information on how to maintain the disorder or improve their current ED behaviors. As mentioned above, the sites state they are not for individuals interested in recovery, but they are supporting those who wish to continue to engage in ED behaviors. Although posts or chats on pro-ana websites may include negative experiences, the tone of these sites ultimately celebrates and supports anorexic and bulimic practices.

One of the greatest dangers of the pro-ana sites is the threat of an eating disorder is physical as well as psychological. Based on research about the users on these sites, assumptions are often challenged and eating disorders are presented as an appealing lifestyle. Users of these sites often consider themselves elite and simply striving for perfection through control of their food intake and their bodies. Professionals are concerned that pro-ana sites provide individuals struggling with an eating disorder with the methods to achieve their goals and perpetuate this body image ideal through an enabling support system that is hidden away from family and friends.

The harm these sites can do is undeniable, and pressure has been exerted on servers to take the pro-ana sites down. While some servers have stopped allowing detected pro-ana sites to operate, others cite First Amendment rights to let them remain. In addition, the pro-ana community finds other ways, such as running diet sites that contain comparable information. Admittedly, these sites were difficult to find during research conducted for this book, but it is impossible to block all pro-ana content, and the information is still available online if someone knows where to look.

INCORPORATION OF EXERCISE INTO TREATMENT OF EATING DISORDERS

Shifting away from societal influences and social media and to the treatment aspect, the next issue and controversy associated with eating disorders are related to the incorporation of exercise into treatment for eating disorders. Incorporating exercise into ED treatment has been forbidden or frowned upon for as long as treatment centers have existed, and it remains controversial. Often exercise is the first thing that patient are asked to eliminate from their life when they enter treatment, because it could be a significant piece of the eating disorder and is "not necessary" (unlike eating) during treatment. While most treatment centers continue to forbid exercise during treatment, some ED centers have started to examine how exercise can be incorporated into treatment. Among the latter, sometimes only walking or yoga is allowed. Other treatment centers—particularly some of the treatment centers who specialize in treating athletes with eating disorders—are learning to incorporate exercise including strength and conditioning, cardio, or even a patient's sport back into their lives. There is an expectation that some patients who have struggled with eating disorders should not ever return to exercising, and this is absolutely the case. There is another group of patients who were unable to exercise during treatment and they might want to return to exercise after treatment, but they may not be able to return to exercise healthfully since it was not incorporated into their treatment. Finally, there are patients who had the opportunity to incorporate exercise into their treatment and are able to understand the role that exercise might have in their life. Unfortunately, it is difficult to say what the best approach to incorporating exercise into treatment truly is!

INSURANCE COVERAGE

One of the last significant issues related to eating disorders has to do with insurance coverage for treatment. In chapter 5, we discussed the various levels of care, but we failed to mention how much all of these treatments cost. There are hundreds of ED treatment centers and treatment providers, ranging from outpatient to inpatient and everything in between across the United States and across the world, but, unfortunately, they often cost substantially. While the majority of treatment centers accept health insurance, it often doesn't cover all the cost. And some treatment centers and most individual treatment providers do not accept health insurance at all. In addition, some of the particular eating disorders are not covered by insurance. For example, binge eating disorder was recently added to the *Diagnostic and Statistical Manual of Mental Disorders* (*DSM*) and is beginning to receive more insurance coverage for treatment, but it hasn't had any historically. There are other eating disorders discussed in chapter 1 (e.g., diabulimia and orthorexia) that are not formally a part of the *DSM* and typically do not receive insurance coverage either. Finally, while some eating disorders are covered by insurance, patients do not always get coverage for the amount of time that they need to properly recover during treatment.

According to a recent study by Frisch and colleagues, who surveyed around 86 percent of treatment centers in the United States, the average length of stay in treatment is 83 days with an average cost per day of $956. Several other resources suggest that the average residential treatment program for eating disorders costs approximately $30,000 a month, and many patients need three or more months of treatment. One prominent treatment center has publicized its rates; it has stated that a partial hospitalization program with its facility (approximately 30 hours a week) costs between $17,000 and $20,000 a month and its intensive outpatient program (approximately 9 hours a week) costs between $7,000 and $10,000 for a six-week period. Research shows this is comparable to most treatment centers in metropolitan areas in the United States. In addition to this cost for higher levels of care, patients often need years of follow-up care, including treatment with a mental health professional, a physician, a nutritionist, and potentially a psychiatrist.

Another controversy around health insurance is the approach that requires that patients attempt outpatient treatment for an eating disorder first and, if they "fail" at the outpatient level, they are allowed to transition to a higher level of care. Recall the risks that were highlighted in chapter 4; failing can be quite dangerous with eating disorders.

This chapter only scratches the surface with some of the issues and controversies related to eating disorders. Societal influences on eating disorders, social media, incorporating exercise into ED treatment, and insurance coverage for eating disorders are just a few of the most significant issues and controversies. There are likely more to come!

10

Current Research and Future Directions

The field of eating disorders is always growing, specifically with fascinating research and new approaches to diagnosing and treating this serious illness. An increased number of genetic studies as well as pharmacological developments have not only assisted many in the helping or support role but also provided more insight and knowledge to those struggling with an eating disorder. These advancements are not just in a lab or centered around particular research studies. In fact, building societal awareness and widespread acceptance for the intensity of this illness has contributed to legislative changes that have positively influenced many individuals struggling with all types of eating disorders. This chapter will highlight some of the genetic research focused on heritability and what we may know about the manifestation of an eating disorder earlier in the process, as well as what changes or improvements, including medications, are on the horizon for helping those with an eating disorder. It will conclude with an extensive look at social change, societal influence, and examples of current legislation encouragingly impacting this area of mental health.

GENETIC FACTORS UNDERLYING AN EATING DISORDER

Increasingly detailed analyses and studies focusing on the influence of genetic factors on the evolution of eating disorders have started to shift the field of eating disorders and expanded our thinking around the origin of an incredibly complex disease. It is important to note that this section is merely a broad overview of some of the studies on genetics but not comprehensive enough to make generalizations for all types of eating disorders and/or symptoms.

Eating disorders have historically been regarded as sociocultural. This means that the origin of the illness was believed to have been rooted in specific practices, beliefs, or ideals that depict a particular group or society. These can change with time as a result of ecological, social, or technological trends or advancements. For example, one may be predisposed to developing an eating disorder due to observation and practice of disordered behaviors starting at a young age within a family, such as only eating "healthy" food. Another example would be appearance standards set by a particular sport culture. These internalized norms become a driving force behind using ED behaviors to look a particular way among the group with the intention of fitting in.

Genetics, on the other hand, refers to the scientific study of heredity. Putting it very simplistically, looking closely at genetics allows us to observe the spread of single genes within families as well as to study more multifaceted types of inheritance. Genetic research has allowed researchers not only to learn more about particular diseases but also to diagnose and treat. While the study of genetics pertaining to eating disorders remains in preliminary stages relative to other fields, there is evidence that biological components play a part when it comes to determining who develops an eating disorder. There is a need to continue providing this same level of investigation, knowledge, and applied practice to the field in order to influence the prevention of ED development. This is promising, considering what has already been uncovered and described in some of the following studies.

Berretini (2004) reviewed various studies focusing on the heritability of eating disorders among relatives. Heritability refers to the amount of variation in a trait that can be credited to genetic factors. First utilizing family studies, he studied rates of eating disorders in those related biologically, such as mother and daughter. While findings suggested increased rates of heritability, twin studies were necessary to parse out environmental causes from those that were truly genetic within a family, since family members share both. These particular twin studies further revealed a significant link between the development of eating disorders and genetic factors. This finding was also true for particular ED symptoms or attitudes, including perfectionism, body dissatisfaction, or intense focus on weight, as well as some comorbid mood disorders. It is important to note that additional research is necessary to analyze and describe the exact genetic discrepancy in more detail.

In his article, Berretini also made sure to point out developmental differences when it came to the genetic influence on the development of an eating disorder. Studies found increased heritability in those who had already gone through puberty compared to those who had not.

When it comes to genetic research and this illness, molecular genetics is one of the more recent areas of observation and research in the field, particularly when focusing on genetic contribution. Molecular genetics, which refers to an examination of the structure and function of genes on a molecular level, can provide more specific recognition for those genes believed to play a significant role in the progression of an eating disorder. How a gene is expressed can provide information about heredity. Klump and Culbert (2007) looked at studies examining the genetic origin of eating disorders. Their findings point to serotonin, brain-derived neurotrophic factor (BDNF), and estrogen genes as three main contributors to the development of this illness; however, they added that the extent of their influence is unknown. Along with much more research, a call for future studies with larger sample sizes and a clearer description of how genes interact with the environment may provide more confirming results.

A more recent study was conducted by researchers at the University of Iowa and the University of Texas Southwestern Medical Center in 2013. Contrary to the more common approach of looking at a large group of participants, these scientists instead looked at individual families with a history of eating disorders throughout generations. Results revealed two genes in particular believed to be responsible for a much higher potential for developing an eating disorder, specifically when gene mutations result in a decreased desire to eat. Michael Lutter explained that these findings will further support investigation of the etiology of eating disorders in order to develop pathways for prevention. This same study also found evidence that these individuals did not display ED symptoms until they were older.

As mentioned in earlier chapters, eating disorders often surface with comorbid conditions. Some of the genetic research has also looked at genetic links among eating disorders and other illnesses, including substance use disorders. In 2013, researchers at the Washington University School of Medicine confirmed shared genetic risk factors between specific ED symptoms and alcohol dependence. The researchers noted that previous studies had encountered similar findings; however, this was the first to include both men and women participants. This was a significant discovery, considering the prevalent comorbidity of both these illnesses. The lead researcher for this study, Melissa A. Munn-Chernoff, has suggested future directions in research involving actual blood and saliva samples to gather more specific identifying information about the genes themselves. Additionally, diversifying the participating population, as well as increasing the sample size within these studies, will help determine the extent of overlap these same findings have among various backgrounds and groups of people.

In terms of future directions for studying genetics and eating disorders, epigenetics is one the most discussed areas. Epigenetics refers to a change in gene expression, not the actual code itself. This area of study looks at certain biological processes that can turn a gene off and on. Yilmaz, Hardaway, and Bulik (2015) broadly describe epigenetics' current role within ED research as focused mainly on DNA methylation. Methylation alters the activity of the DNA rather than the DNA sequence. Yilmaz, Hardaway, and Bulik recommend future research to expand beyond DNA methylation and, instead, incorporate other epigenetic mechanisms.

PHARMACOLOGICAL ADVANCEMENTS FOR THE TREATMENT OF EATING DISORDERS

Research has shown that the combination of medication and psychotherapy often offers one of the more encouraging outcomes in terms of prognosis moving forward in the treatment of an eating disorder. Historically however, there has been more literature on the impact of psychotherapy, or talk therapy, for the treatment of eating disorders than of pharmacological interventions.

Many co-occurring issues and symptoms, sometimes resulting from an eating disorder, are commonly treated with medications if it is determined that this will benefit the recovery of the individual. Medications prescribed to combat mood symptoms paralleling or worsening the progression of an eating disorder can be beneficial at all stages of the illness. Anxiety and depression are two of the more common comorbid disorders often treated with atypical antipsychotics and antidepressants. There are also prescribed medications intended to alleviate some of the physical symptoms that accompany the discomfort of moving away from ED behaviors, such as stomach upset, nausea, and sleep disturbance.

It is important to note that not all cases referred to ED treatment require medications. In fact, there are many people challenged with less severe cases who enter recovery without the implementation or trial of any psychotropic intervention. Medication can also be recommended and encouraged in order to help individuals maintain their own safety as well.

In their article focusing on the pharmacological treatment of eating disorders, Gorla and Matthews (2005) point out that the stigma around psychotherapy, as well as the shortage of trained professionals, limits interest in pursuing psychotherapy; therefore, medical professionals, such as family doctors and pediatricians, are sometimes the only treating provider for someone struggling. Medications then become the primary form of intervention, which is another reason why medical professionals should be well informed in the treatment of eating disorder. As highlighted in an earlier chapter, there is strong need for more training specifically around eating disorders in medical school curricula. Currently, the recommended treatment for this illness remains a combination of psychotropic medication and therapy, not just medicinal interventions.

There are some medications recommended specifically to combat symptoms of an eating disorder. For example, Zyprexa, which is a mood stabilizer, can also aid in weight restoration. This property makes it difficult for some to adhere to consistently. Zyprexa is an example of a medication that must be monitored closely in order to ensure that restoration is not occurring only because of the medication. If this were the case, true evidence for one's ability to interrupt behaviors could be in question and potentially hinder a positive long-term prognosis.

It is important to be an informed consumer when it comes to medications that are advertised as moderating appetite. The Food and Drug Administration (FDA) has approved some of these medications to be used alongside the recommendation of a prescribing clinician, but there are also many on the market that are not approved, thus making them unsafe and risky to use. Of the medications prescribed to impact appetite, it is commonly recommended that the prescriptions be taken in conjunction with therapy, behavior change, and ongoing consultation with a dietician to address diet and exercise. These drugs can be tempting for those struggling with an eating disorder, especially one that includes restriction. This can easily lead especially to increased medical or psychological risk.

Serotonin and norepinephrine are two of the neurotransmitters in the brain that impact many things, including appetite and hunger. Prescribing clinicians may consider the role of these neurotransmitters and particular interactions, alongside the eating disorder and mood symptoms, when it comes to recommending a particular medication.

When it comes to medications, antidepressants, such as fluoxetine, also known as Prozac, are commonly used to address the bulimic symptoms of eating disorder. Gorla and Matthews (2005) and Couturier and Lock's (2007) work specifically with children and adolescents are two examples of research that highlight success with medications when treating bulimia nervosa, specifically decreasing the binge-and-purge episodes. A few of the cases studied within Couturier and Lock's research, on both children and adults, also supported the use of atypical antipsychotics for treating anxiety in those struggling with anorexia nervosa. Guido Frank highlighted findings in his 2016 case series that supports aripiprazole, a more commonly known antipsychotic medication called Abilify, and its ability to lessen fear for those in treatment for anorexia nervosa. Reports from the article highlight reports of decreased anxiety, which contributed to letting go of behaviors centered upon specific fears. There is a widespread call for further examination into the use of medications when treating eating disorders, specifically for studies that incorporate longer-term analysis.

SOCIETAL AWARENESS OF EATING DISORDERS AND MOVEMENT TOWARD SOCIAL CHANGE

With ongoing technological advancements and the ability to reach so many more people, social media is an avenue that the field of eating disorders is constantly navigating, growing with, and using to implement constructive change. Photos, posts, and interactive dialogue are only a few of the ways this social wave of communication and connection can have both effective and harmful influences over those involved with eating disorders, really in any capacity. If implemented in a positive, proactive, and inclusive manner, social media can strongly impact societal awareness and reach many people.

Efforts to use social media as a platform for encouraging recovery has significantly changed within the past few years. Not only are more individuals using their own experiences through social media to raise awareness but treatment programs, hospitals, and larger-scale groups also have more of a social presence. Online support groups and websites now serve as outlets that are much more visible and influential to more people, both for those who have disordered eating or an eating disorder, but also for those in a supportive role. For individuals more fearful of in-person interactions or who have less time to travel, participation in an online support group can be a helpful tool for joining community, gaining more recovery skills, and implementing structure into one's routine. This influence can be inspiring to many who are struggling, as well as those already working toward recovery.

There is always a flip side to the positive impact of an online presence and growing technology. It is very important to be aware of the websites that do not support recovery and, instead, promote ED behaviors as mentioned in chapter 9. While they may seem to provide a sense of community, it can be devastating when individuals use this type of support to become further connected to their illness. Additionally, while not always intended to do so, many websites and social media accounts only show what is assumed to be the ideal physical image or appearance. Many times, these pictures have already been photoshopped and edited, further presenting an unattainable and false representation of one's body. Without the normalization of all body sizes, shapes, and presentations, an impossible and distorted image is created that many try to attain through the use of disordered eating and exercise behaviors. Luckily, there are a growing number of websites, some of which will be mentioned later in the chapter, and social media accounts combating these distorted images and working to normalize acceptance for any physique. The Health at Every Size® (HAES) approach, which is trademarked by the Association for Size Diversity and Health, is an example of a growing movement intended to eliminate size discrimination. The HAES approach and associated principles aim to illuminate the idea that health includes not just physical attributes but also other aspects—such as social, emotional, spiritual, relational, and intellectual—of one's well-being. This organization holds an annual conference and implements educational webinars and online resources to provide more information about the organization and its ideals. It is important for ideals around physical appearance, such as thinness, to be changed in order to support healthier and more stable relationships between individuals and their bodies, which would ultimately reduce the prevalence of disordered eating behaviors and eating disorders.

Social Change

Treatment intended to interrupt the behaviors and actions driving one's illness are essential, but it is only one part of empowering recovery. The environmental influences that one is surrounded by daily call for sociocultural change. This is to ensure that the people one seeks validation and acceptance from do not focus solely on equating physical appearance with self-worth. For this reason, it is important to look at traditions, values, beliefs, and the like that make up a group of people or sector of society and evaluate the influence they may have on predisposing one to unhealthy thoughts or furthering one's ED behaviors.

Social change can present in many forms. A few examples of these avenues include, but are not limited to, rallies, groups settings, and government petitioning. Equally important is the effort put forth by individuals to empower movement away from particular beliefs about beauty and appearance, as well as from the use of behaviors intended to attain feeling loved, included, worthy, and accepted. This requires gaining knowledge and spending time building awareness about the intricacies of an eating disorder.

It is important to recognize that eating disorders do not discriminate. People of all genders, religions, sexualities, socioeconomic statues, and ethnic backgrounds are susceptible to developing all types of disordered eating behaviors and/or eating disorders. Historically, as shown earlier, eating disorders were viewed as a disease that mainly impacted women; however, this is no longer the case. One-third of people struggling with an eating disorder are male, but, partly because of bias and stigma, less of them seek treatment. More prevalent societal levels of body acceptance and self-worth could help change the tide when it comes to the development of ED symptoms.

As mentioned above, there are many groups and organizations, with social media presence, working to raise awareness about eating disorders while simultaneously enacting change. One example of this is McCall Dempsey's work to create Southern Smash, which has become one of the best-known avenues for support in the realm of eating disorders. Southern Smash encourages individuals to shift how they define themselves and their worth through college campus events, public speaking engagements, blogging, media appearances, and, most notably, their scale smashing events.

Another example of intervention aimed to create social change with regard to unreasonable and impractical beauty and appearance ideals is the Body Project. The Body Project was originally developed by researchers at Stanford University, the University of Texas at Austin, and the Oregon Research Institute. This group-based platform has provided an opportunity for more than one million individuals to connect and engage through written, verbal, and/or experiential exercises centered around connecting with a more authentic and healthier body image. The platform helps not only to recognize the influence of social pressure but also to take a stand against it. Many studies have shown connection between the Body Project and a decrease in the development of eating disorders.

Specific beliefs and views about how one's body should look may put someone at a higher risk for developing an eating disorder. These beliefs start at a very young age, often due to society's pressure and encouragement to diet as well as to role models for behaviors within family systems. There is an alarming percentage of children, some as young as age 10, who have been exposed to dieting behaviors or attempted to diet themselves. This reality highlights the need for greater awareness of how children conceptualize their bodies as well as the extent to which they will go to change their appearance in order to be seen in a more positive way by peers or family members. Bullying and rejection behaviors centered around weight are just one example where society has power to shift the correlation between body image and worth.

This trend is especially prominent in sport due to the pressure to look a certain way in order to perform at one's peak performance level. Awareness of when and where this is occurring, as well as efforts to empower people to look past physical appearance to be seen as successful and worthy, are essential when it comes to influencing social behavior and relations.

Change can occur specifically within sports that involve cutting weight, such as wrestling, boxing, or rowing, as well as those that place strong emphasis on the aesthetic nature of a sport, such as gymnastics or figure skating. Team culture and the associated values are crucial areas of focus because of the power they hold in molding each athlete's belief around what is expected or viewed as important, especially when it comes to a particular weight, shape, or size. Shifting the focus away from valuing physical appearance and instead centering upon other components of the sport that do not require engaging in destructive behaviors is one example of tackling the negative impact body image can have in sport. Additionally, challenging society's push for a certain physique can help one steer away from aspiring to achieve perfectionism at the expense of health. Making social change requires improving one's self-efficacy and confidence.

LEGISLATIVE CHANGES RELATED TO EATING DISORDERS

Legislation is a broad term; however, in the case of eating disorders, it often entails a desire for change enacted though regulation, funding, or some type of declaration or an act. Prior to a shift like this being formally confirmed, the desired change may be expressed in many forms. These may include written propositions, group gatherings, or meetings, such as rallies, that are all related to the proposed bill, funding, or act that is intended to eventually be passed or approved. Often the expected outcome of change is fueled by an event in the past or repeated trend that is no longer working or helping those struggling.

The first-ever eating disorders legislation was the Anna Westin Act of 2015. Anna Westin developed anorexia at age 16. She sought outpatient care and was believed to be on the path toward recovery. At 18, she relapsed with more severe and persistent behaviors, and the clinical and medical recommendation was immediate inpatient hospitalization. Anna Westin committed suicide in 2000 shortly after insurance denied coverage for a higher level of care after her anorexia nervosa worsened. Anna's mom, Kitty Westin, has spent countless years and effort working to prevent other parents and their children from having to endure the unfortunate sequence of tragic events involving insurance for treatment coverage. She started the Anna Westin Foundation, now known as WithAll (formerly the Emily Program Foundation).

In 2002, the Anna Westin House was opened. This was the first residential ED program in Minnesota. Since then, many residential houses have become essential components to treatment programs.

In 2016, the Anna Westin Act was passed by Congress and the Senate under the 21st Century Cures Act and was signed by President Barack Obama. This law provided more funding for health-care professionals and school personnel with the intention of enabling earlier intervention strategies and action. An additional goal of this legislation was to amplify coverage by insurance companies, including residential costs.

Another example of ED legislation is the LIVE Well Act, a health-centered act that would also include attention toward ED prevention. This act focuses on health instead of just weight, and it aims to identify those at risk for developing disordered eating behaviors and/or an eating disorder. With support, the hope is to provide prevention grants for schools and other programs in the community. Participation related to this movement is again through NEDA, but the grants are funded through the US Department of Agriculture.

Various ED foundations or organizations, such as NEDA, are examples of constant endorsement and organization of proposed change. Advocates from NEDA work to increase awareness about eating disorders, prevention, and treatment access, as well as to encourage more funding for ED research and advancements. Advocates include those working on a volunteer basis but also some people who work for the government. NEDA attempts to ease the process of proposing change and sharing thoughts with lawmakers by providing information on its website for how to contact lawmakers. These organizations are also always encouraging and inviting people to become involved as advocates in order to bring more voices together in this field. Advocates can include professionals, family members, those struggling with an eating disorder, or really anyone who has been touched or influenced by this illness.

The Eating Disorders Coalition (EDC) is another avenue for building awareness among politicians and proposing new congressional bills aimed at advocating and providing greater access to treatment for those with an eating disorder. The EDC has also joined advocacy efforts to improve current health policies. Its goals center on further prioritizing eating disorders as a public health issue and helping to fund resources that would initiate more education and prevention opportunities. It also has a presence on social media that helps build awareness and provide a platform to share information about its current policy work and advancements.

The EDC consistently has a variety of events or initiatives in motion that are often open to anyone who would like to become involved. One example of the coalition's work related to enacting change was hosting a pediatric ED training for primary care providers. This is especially significant because of the consistent drive to include more dedicated education and knowledge about eating disorders in medical school curricula and to ensure compliance and direction around what is being taught in the ED elective or rotation. Another example was its push for more funding in the military that is specifically allotted for ED research. The EDC pointed out the prevalence of at-risk cadets and the consequent need for access to treatment. Over the past two decades, there have been numerous initiatives put into place and acts passed that are specific to ED awareness, prevention, and treatment. This offers hope for more movement and support ahead.

As you can see, there has been a tremendous amount of movement when it comes to building awareness and advocating for necessary changes in this field—all intended to save more lives. The good news is that as the stigma around having an eating disorder continues to slowly decline, there will be more time, resources, and people available and willing to further enact change and ideas intended to propel even more knowledge around the identification and treatment of eating disorders.

Case Illustrations

GABRIELLE

Gabrielle is a 16-year-old female currently struggling with anorexia nervosa, restrictive type. She is completing her sophomore year of high school at a new school due to recently transferring after her freshman year. During this first year of high school, she experienced significant difficulty making friends and was often bullied and teased for her appearance and clothing style. She takes honors classes for both science and math while also participating on the school's speech and debate team and annual theatre production. She has acknowledged a strong desire to fit in socially and to find a greater level of connection with her peers both in and out of school. As a result, she has recently started comparing herself to some of the other students she has viewed as "popular" since her first day at the new school. Gabrielle has always struggled with self-confidence, but specifically in terms of body image thoughts and critique of herself. She also fears others are frequently judging her, based on evidence of earlier bullying. Historically, she has never felt thin enough and has been berated by her mom, who also struggles with disordered eating patterns. When Gabrielle makes comments about her weight, they are often reaffirmed and followed up with proposed ideas to lose weight from her mom. Previously, she never engaged in any long-term restricting or other ED behaviors, but she has grown up in a household where "clean eating" and a narrow list of food choices are consistently encouraged. Gabrielle began researching ways to lose weight and has started to experiment with cutting calories and reducing portions. She is more frequently swapping some of her normal food choices, such as chips, with what she believes are "healthier" items, like fruit and salads. Her portions sizes have also decreased as she starts to eat half the servings she previously did. Gabrielle revels in the gradual weight loss as the compliments from friends and family start coming in daily. The attention fuels even more stricter eating to the point of eliminating full meals and avoiding events that would involve eating, such as holiday meals, birthday parties, and social engagement centered around eating out together at a restaurant. There is constant attention on her body from herself and others as well as a strong desire to continue losing more weight. She feels as though the only way she will make friends is if she is in a smaller body, thus placing significant importance and value around the number on the scale and size of her clothing. Like many who struggle with anorexia, Gabrielle continues to lower her weight marker each time she hits a goal, often encouraging herself with statements like, "Only five more pounds." The control over the loud thoughts and the temporary relief that comes from achieving what she believes will help her attain connection has kept her in the illness much longer than anticipated. It has also brought her closer to a routine of loneliness and fixation on food. Ironically, the more she restricts her food and disallows involvement with events or experiences including food, the more isolated she becomes. This is the opposite of what she initially intended to happen by experimenting with ED behaviors, and now she is fully entrenched in her illness. She is starting to notice its effect other areas of life, including her studies and performance events. She has difficulty paying attention in class, retaining the material, and memorizing her lines for the upcoming play. Her family has also experienced her with less energy and fogginess in the brain during their more limited interactions. Gabrielle seems to be somewhat checked out and avoidant of much interaction with them or the few friends she has connected to at school. As her weight drops below what is appropriate for someone her age, developmental level, and height, she has also started to experience some of the hallmark physical signs of an eating disorder as she plummets further into it: exhaustion, changes in the strength of her nails and hair, dizziness, fatigue, and mild cold intolerance. Despite her family and friends now starting to notice more of these consequences, she remains defensive and minimizes her struggle when they express concern or offer support. The more people work to get closer, the more Gabrielle pushes them away in order to spend time cultivating her relationship with her eating disorder.

Analysis

Gabrielle's narrative highlights a common precursor to developing anorexia nervosa as well as a usual trajectory of events leading to greater fusion with this illness. While each individual presentation varies in some regard, the progression of denial ("I'm fine!"), firm belief her behaviors are "normal," and eventual isolation away from friends and family are all frequently observed components of this illness. As described in chapter 1,

Gabrielle meets criteria for anorexia nervosa, restrictive type due to her efforts to decrease her intake, resulting in significantly low body weight, expressed fear of weight gain, and a distorted and negative body image. Additionally, Gabrielle's lack of awareness for the severity of her struggle is an indicator for not only having an eating disorder but also allowing it to take greater control of her daily functioning and overall health. Gabrielle's body mass index (BMI) remains above 16, which would warrant a current severity level of "moderate." This is another reason that immediate support toward interrupting her behaviors could propel a more hopeful prognosis instead of reaching an even more worrisome place physically and psychologically.

Individual therapy and participation in an adolescent support group may offer Gabrielle the space to connect with others enduring similar struggles as well as open up about past and current events influencing her use of ED behaviors. This may illuminate the need to further evaluate her social influences and potential need for boundaries. As far as the function of her ED behaviors, there are many possibilities. Gabrielle could be using her restriction to feel more in control when all other realms of her life—specifically, fitting in with her peers—feel so distant. Another drive for remaining connected to her disorder could be resistance to the feelings accompanying these distressing experiences. For example, she could be using restriction to mask and distance herself from embarrassment, sadness, loneliness, and so forth.

It would be important for Gabrielle's parents and primary care doctor to determine whether outpatient level of care is sufficient at this time or if another option, as mentioned in chapter 5, is more appropriate. Finally, it would be beneficial for her family to participate in and utilize some of the many available resources described throughout the book that are intended to inform and support those navigating the caretaking role on behalf of someone working to recover.

BETSY

Betsy is a 54-year-old female who recently retired from holding a senior position within the same tech company for almost 20 years. She is currently living with her husband, younger daughter, who is getting ready to finish her senior of high school, and two dogs. She has one other daughter, who is currently in college. Betsy's family has always been close-knit and enjoyed doing many things together, including traveling, skiing, cooking, and other activities. When her first daughter left for college, Betsy experienced sadness and a change in her routine; however, she was still working, and her younger daughter and husband kept the household busy and lively.

Betsy has always experienced increased focus and perseverance on her weight. Starting in college, she was regularly experimenting with the newest fad diet. Consequently, her weight yo-yoed as she struggled to find any consistency in eating normally, moving her body a moderate amount, and listening to her authentic hunger and fullness cues.

More recently, as the thought of both daughters leaving her home has surfaced, Betsy is beginning to turn to food as a way to cope. What started as intermittent grazing in between meals or going back for additional helpings has slowly led to intentional and planned binge episodes. Her change in routine and structure has signaled a significant life transition; many changes are occurring all at once. Any discussion or planning revolving around her daughter's upcoming move more frequently instigates intense sadness, isolation, and, consequently, more frequent periods of time spent eating unusually large quantities of food in secret. Betsy is starting to feel more out of control and uncomfortably full after almost every period of binge eating. Her typical binge foods include dinner leftovers, cookies, ice cream, whole pizzas, cereal, and trail mix. Guilt following the nightly binges has led to some restriction earlier in the day. Betsy skips most breakfasts and lunches but does attempt to eat dinner with her husband and daughter. She is becoming more frustrated as these periods of restriction during the day fuel intense hunger cues and drives to binge later in the evening as well as closer to midnight, after the rest of her family have gone to bed.

Betsy's husband is unaware of the extent of her behaviors but has started to ask about the noticeable changes in her meal routine as well as the unexplained expenses on their credit card from various grocery stores and gas stations. Betsy denies cause for concern partly because of her own denial and partly because of the shame and embarrassment.

With regard to previous ED behaviors, Betsy often has an intense focus on her body image and spends more time than normal calculating calories and tracking her weight trend. She has never pursued a particular regimen that would be classified as a diagnosable eating disorder but has experimented for short periods of time with various restrictive fad diets, fasting attempts in her younger years, and most recently, the elimination of carbohydrates and some fats from her intake. While Betsy experimented with purging in college, she is not currently engaging in this behavior or using any substances or medications that could have a laxative or diuretic affect. She has noticed increasing difficulty listening to her hunger cues and practicing any sort of intuitive eating habits because of the growing emotional connection to her behaviors.

Analysis

When looking at Betsy's case from a clinical perspective, it is important to consider her lengthy history of using food and specific disordered behaviors as a way to manage, cope with, or numb her feelings revolving around her current major life transition, as well as a potential sense of loss as she and her husband become empty nesters. This would indicate that just guidance alone around a meal plan will not be sufficient in helping her interrupt her eating disorder. Instead, direction around appropriate amounts of food, reevaluation of hunger and fullness cues, and timing of her intake should parallel individual therapy and dietary counseling at the minimum. Betsy would benefit from time spent redefining what her marriage with husband will look like moving ahead as well as exploring the most effective ways of remaining connected to her daughters as they embark on a new path in their lives. When appropriate, this component of her work will entail processing the associated grief related to leaving her career, as well as saying good-bye to her daughters. Additionally, group therapy would be a very useful outlet for Betsy to take part in, in order to feel less alone. Often, binge behaviors can be a way to fill a void or sense of emptiness. Therefore, connecting with others who can relate may help Betsy move closer to the emotional experience of retirement and separation from her daughters and away from maladaptive coping.

With regard to specific treatment modalities, dialectical behavior therapy (DBT) would be an ideal, empirically supported option as it focuses initially on changing behaviors. Betsy would be encouraged and supported around developing skills, as described in chapter 5, to replace her harmful ED patterns, specifically bingeing. She would focus on the use of mindfulness, interpersonal effectiveness, emotion regulation, and distress tolerance. Ideally, these skills would help Betsy shift the time spent in her eating disorder to improving her relationships with her family and friends as well as focus more on the present moment and her current needs. Restructuring her daily routine and activities will require reevaluation of values and interests that do not involve her eating disorder. This is an essential step toward maintaining a life in recovery.

As noted extensively throughout the book, while not intentional, the impact Betsy's illness has on her husband and daughters can be serious. It is crucial that they are able to also access and participate in some form of support group or therapy setting. Betsy's eating disorder is not only affecting the family dynamics but is also being influenced by the family system; therefore, some form of change will likely be required by all members.

CHRISTY

Christy is a 19-year-old female currently living with her three college roommates in an on-campus dorm suite. Two of these three roommates are also teammates of hers on the gymnastics team. She just finished her first set of exams after returning from a long holiday break at home and is gradually settling into the routine of life as a student-athlete. Christy has endured an impressive athletic career that started at age three, when she was enrolled in a toddler gymnastics class. Christy's development and expressed enjoyment for this sport has exponentially grown as her life, travel, and social community have increasingly revolved around high-level gymnastics. However, her transition into her collegiate career on the university's Division I gymnastics team has contributed to significant struggle with restriction, overexercise, focus on appearance, and fixation around calories.

Throughout high school, Christy was often fielding comments centered upon ideal body image and expectations for performance. Not only did this pressure to look a particular way feel overwhelming but also her fear of not living up to her coaches' and parents' expectations magnified as she quickly moved upward in the gymnastics ranks. She watched teammates, competitors, and coaches act as role models for disordered behaviors and various dieting behaviors while talking in a way that solidified her belief that a lighter and more toned body equated to better performance. She consistently convinced herself that cutting out particular food groups deemed as "unhealthy" or "bad," as well as disallowing any type of day off for rest, was merely part of this sport's norm and the lifestyle of a collegiate gymnast.

Christy's rigidity with food and excessive exercise outside her prescribed workouts and practices has wavered throughout her career; however, she was consistently able to stay within a weight range appropriate *enough* to continue competing and not warrant expressed concern from others. Additionally, while many of her food choices became geared to what would be considered as orthorexic or "clean," she was able to consume enough calories to sustain her required mental and physical energy. It was not until the end of her senior year of high school, as she began to connect more with the pressure of upcoming college gymnastics, that her already narrow range of food options, small portion sizes, and intense focus on her body weight became unwavering. Christy's typical day has slowly become built around runs and extra lifting sessions outside of her already demanding schedule of team practice, conditioning, class, and tutoring. Her food choices mostly consist of salads and chicken, with an occasional protein bar before a practice. This increasingly inflexible planning has started to unfold at the expense of plans with others and time dedicated to studying as her exercise and control around food have now taken precedence. Additionally, Christy's attention has become consumed by her obsession to lose more weight. Despite reaching her disordered weight loss goals, it has yet to feel like enough, and she is slowly compromising health in pursuit of becoming smaller. Christy is constantly looking at herself in mirrors, windows, and reflective surfaces seeking reassurance but very rarely feeling satisfied with what she sees.

Christy's sports medicine team has flagged her as a student athlete to keep an eye on due to ongoing weight loss, isolation from the team, and an overall decrease in positive emotions. Her isolation from her team has prevented accountability and enabled more time in her ED behaviors. While she has not been completely removed from practices or preseason competitions, her athletic trainer and coaches have noticed more frequent and uncharacteristic mistakes in her routines as well as a decrease in her ability to maintain enough energy to last throughout practice. As they see her more often, they have also noticed ongoing weight loss that is sparking greater concern.

Analysis

As mentioned at various points throughout the text, Christy's progression with her eating disorder is quite common in the athletic world, especially at the level she is currently competing at. Further, the sport of gymnastics presents additional risk factors that predispose someone to the development of an eating disorder because of the increased focus on aesthetics, revealing uniforms that contribute to increased focus on body image, and a scoring component that naturally draws more evaluation and attention to appearance in addition to her performance. As Christy has experienced more comparison and competition among others, mainly teammates and competitors, her rigidity with behaviors has become more consistent and controlling of her routine. The eating disorder does a stellar job at masking the severity of the illness as it progresses; therefore, denial is a frequent reaction when others express concern or curiosity about noticeable changes. In this situation, the more attention she receives, the more secretive and manipulative Christy's behaviors will become in order to hold onto some form of control.

At some point, it is likely that her athletic personnel team and/or coach will soon set more concrete, measurable, and time-specific goals intended to turn her behaviors around. However, if her eating disorder progresses and puts her at even greater risk, both physically and psychologically, a higher level of care may be mandated and she will have to take a leave from school and sport. One of the goals will be fully interrupting exercise for a period of time in order to help Christy reintegrate sport in a healthy and sustainable way. There are situations where a more intermediate step of meeting with an outpatient team through the university could also be attempted; however, the progression of Christy's behaviors has been fast and unwavering, which is preventing additional time to wait and see what she is able to do at this point.

It would be important to evaluate her current support system. Ideally, this phase of her college journey would be a time for building connection and cohesion with the team, but Christy is fostering the exact opposite. As her relationship with her eating disorder grows, her isolation and distance from her teammates does as well. This detachment has made it difficult for her teammates and support personnel to approach her with their concerns. If possible, the goal would be for Christy to make the decision herself to seek support in interrupting her eating disorder. If this were to occur, her prognosis would be more favorable. Recommending support groups with other student athletes may offer relatedness and connection that sway her in the direction of separating her eating disorder from her authentic self. While this may be later in the journey, this exploration will hopefully entail looking at other parts of her identity that do not involve gymnastics in order to help her look more closely at who she is outside of sport. Due to Christy's history of avoiding conflict and putting others needs before her own, exploration around ways her current presentation is masking misalignment with her true passions and personality would be useful.

One therapeutic approach that could be effective for Christy is acceptance and commitment therapy, also referenced in the book as ACT. Implementing ACT into her work could help Christy identify her core values and commit to creating goals that fulfill them. Instead of shifting thoughts or feelings, the goal would be to help her change her actions and interrupt her pattern of responding to discomfort with restriction and/or exercise. This could shed light on many variables potentially influencing her illness. These may include, but not be limited to, exploring whether sport is enabling her eating disorder, processing sport as an experience she truly wants to continue in a healthy way or terminate from, and looking at how her family relationships and expectations interfere with authentic self-expression. There are many other variables not discussed in this narrative that could play a role in her illness; therefore, commitment and engagement in the therapy process are essential.

CHARLIE

Charlie is a 29-year-old man currently struggling with bulimia nervosa and alcohol use. As a child, Charlie was a strong academic as well as an athlete and a musician. He played multiple sports, was a member of a choir, and played several instruments. Charlie was always physically fit and was only allowed to eat "healthy" foods (no "junk food" or desserts) growing up. He was also never allowed to drink alcohol, and he rarely spent time with friends (and parties were out of the question!) because he needed to focus on his studies and his extracurricular activities. As high school graduation approached, Charlie decided to focus exclusively on his music and settled on the violin while still strumming on the guitar outside of the school orchestra. Charlie went to college to pursue music and graduated with a degree in music studies. He has taught music lessons occasionally, but he really wants to play music, so he is no longer teaching. Currently, Charlie is working as a bartender at a local pizzeria while dreaming about becoming a professional musician. He sings lead in his band and plays guitar several nights and weekends each week. Charlie loves working at the pizzeria because he was never allowed to have pizza as a child. Sometimes, he finds himself eating pizza for breakfast, lunch, and dinner. Lately, he has found himself bingeing on pizza and other "junk" food because it makes him feel free. Charlie has started to notice weight gain with all of the "junk food," though, and he has started going back to the gym. At one point, Charlie was spending nearly two to three hours on the treadmill and/or the elliptical and was feeling as though he was effectively managing his weight. Eventually, Charlie ended up with a stress fracture from all of the tine on those machines, and he has been unable to exercise. Concerned about his weight, Charlie started cutting back on the pizza and other "junk food." He was really frustrated that he wasn't able to eat the way that he wanted or exercise the way that he wanted, so he started drinking more alcohol. He started to rationalize that he could save his calories for drinking and cut his meals to once a day. Finding himself hungry, he often binges on whatever he can find but then feels terrible about it. One night after drinking 12 to 14 beers as well as multiple mixed drinks, he vomited and immediately felt better. Waking up the next morning, he hypothesized that he must have lost most of the calories he consumed. He immediately binged on leftover pizza that he had forbidden himself to eat, and he vomited. Charlie quickly fell into this cycle of bingeing and purging via vomiting to get rid of the calories. He also continued to drink more, because it would typically cause him to vomit. Charlie thought he was effectively managing his weight with the purging while still being able to eat and drink what he wanted, but he was embarrassed about the vomiting and became more isolated. He spends a lot of his days counting calories and finding more successful ways to purge his calories. He has started to skip some of the gigs with his band because it would be too difficult to continue to manage his behaviors at some of the venues. His bandmates are becoming increasingly concerned with his behavior.

Analysis

Unfortunately, Charlie fell into a cycle that is frequently predictable following a childhood that had such rigid rules around food. It is not to say that eating healthy foods or forbidding alcohol during childhood and adolescence can lead to the misuse of food and alcohol later in life, but this likely has been playing into his need to control these things now—especially since the binges are exclusive to the foods that he was unable to eat and the alcohol he was unable to drink. As far as the purging, Charlie actually started purging via exercise as he attempted to manage his weight with two to three hours on the treadmill and/or elliptical, so it also was not surprising that he found another way to purge after his injury. Purging in any form is seemingly effective for the first time or two, which is often reinforcing, but it becomes quickly ineffective and actually backfires shortly thereafter. Therapeutically, it would be imperative for Charlie to recognize and understand what is driving the need to control food and alcohol intake (presumably the inability to control it as a child or adolescent). As mentioned in the case example above, DBT would be an ideal and empirically supported option as it focuses initially on changing behaviors. And as mentioned above and in chapter 5, Charlie needs to develop skills to replace the maladaptive ED patterns—bingeing and purging in this case—that would focus on the use of mindfulness, interpersonal effectiveness, emotion regulation, and distress tolerance. Ideally, these skills would help Charlie reengage in his life and return to doing what he loves: music.

SANDRA

Sandra is a 44-year-old female currently working as an 8th-grade science teacher. She has a 22-year-old daughter named Susan who has been struggling with anorexia nervosa for the last five years of her life. While Sandra does not currently or historically identify as having an eating disorder herself, she has watched her daughter deteriorate physically and psychologically due to AN. Sandra often blames herself and wonders where she went wrong with Susan, especially since she has been on her own after getting a divorce when Susan was five years old. She and her ex-husband had two other daughters; however, neither of them struggled with an eating disorder or any type of body image issues. Sandra has supported her daughter throughout multiple interruptions of school, work, and most recently, an official medical withdrawal from college. During Susan's most recent inpatient treatment episode, Sandra was able to take some time away from work and attend all of the family therapy sessions. Not only did this involvement elicit more self-blame and fear about her daughter's prognosis but also she continually felt as though she could be doing more. Sandra has recently taken a leave from her teaching position to more closely support Susan. This has induced fears about financial instability and greater isolation, as she is distanced from her community of friends, coworkers, and students. Susan's roller coaster of motivation and moments on the road to recovery are almost always followed up with slips and lapses back into old ways of thinking and behaviors. Sandra's life has started to emotionally parallel Susan's experience and days of uncertainty. As Susan has become increasingly more secretive, her lying and dishonesty to Sandra about engaging in ED behaviors has negatively influenced their relationship as well. Sandra is holding onto hope that Susan will eventually find a way to get well, which will also support her longing for the family dynamics to shift back to a place of calm and connection. Sandra is determined to continue attending family therapy with Susan as well as assist her with all her meals and provide the needed support and accountability.

Analysis

While it will likely be advantageous to attend family therapy and support Susan with her meal completion and behavior interruption, it remains imperative that Sandra have support outlets and resources in place for herself. As mentioned in chapter 7, eating disorders can have a significant impact on family and friends, and there are many avenues of individual and group support available. Susan's illness has devastated Sandra and flipped her world upside down. In order for Sandra to support Susan, she will need to engage in her own self-care, set boundaries with Susan, and implement self-compassion in order to stay afloat in the battle she is also enduring. Scheduling time and events with friends will ideally help her balance energy and effort toward maintaining her own social connections while still incorporating time dedicated to Susan. Additionally, Sandra would benefit from attending individual therapy to address her own reactions and emotions to her daughter's illness as well as to have a place to discuss her own self-care and needs. Support groups for family members of individuals with eating disorders would be a great place for Sandra to feel less alone and experience some level of relatedness and understanding. The idea of having to find and balance all of this added support, in addition to what is centered around Susan, is expectedly anxiety-provoking and uncertain. The good news is that there are many organizations and groups specifically intended for those in the support role. Chapters 7 and 8 have outlined and detailed numerous examples, such as NEDA, available for Sandra to connect with.

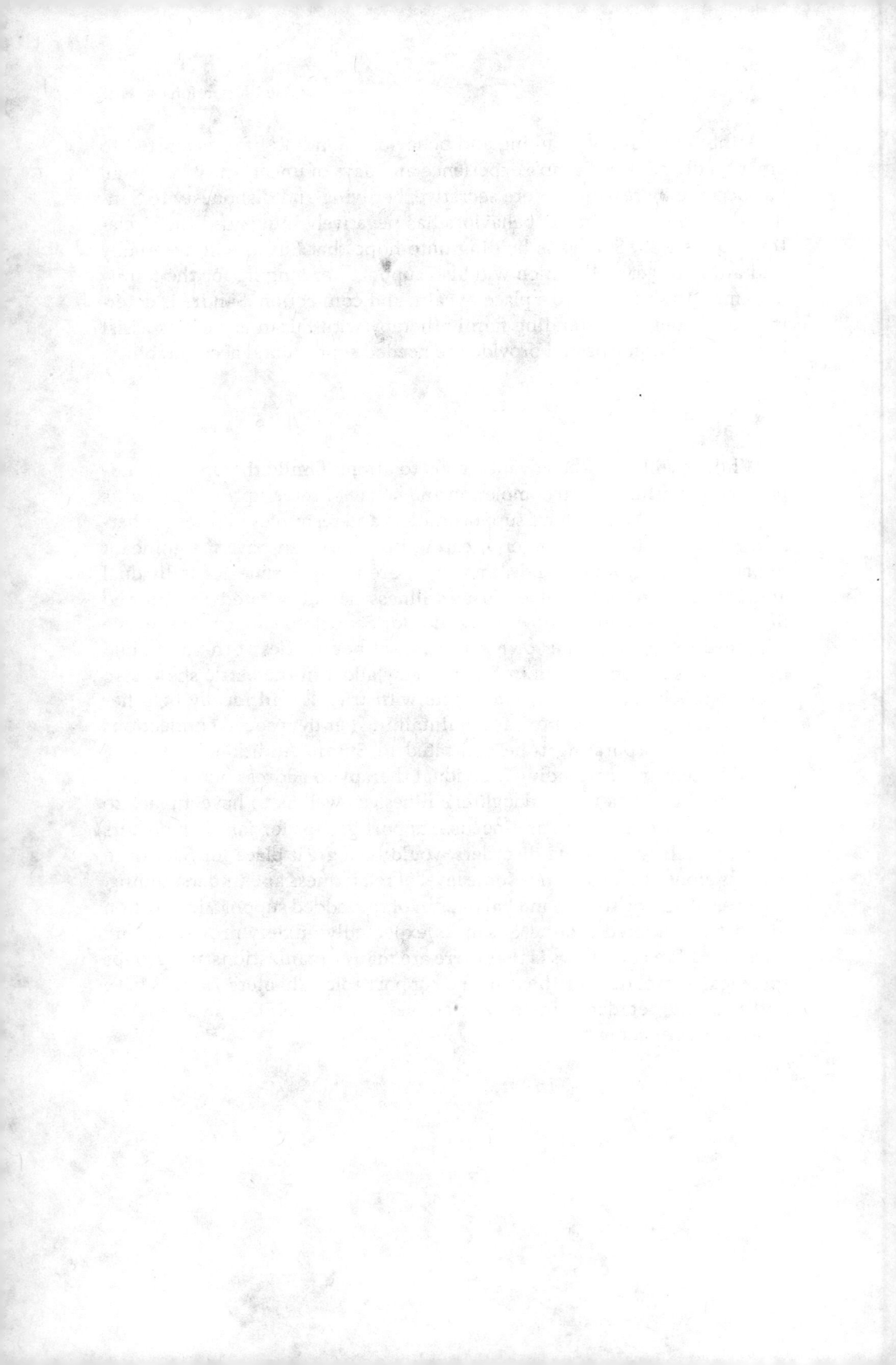

Glossary

Acceptance and commitment therapy (ACT)
Therapy approach focused on changing actions as opposed to changing thoughts and feelings. Individuals are taught to identify core values and commit to creating goals that fulfill these values. ACT also encourages individuals to detach from emotions and learn that pain and anxiety are a normal part of life.

Alkaline phosphatase
ALP is an enzyme found in several tissues throughout the body. The highest concentrations of ALP are present in the cells that make up bones and the liver. Elevated levels of ALP in the blood are most commonly caused by liver disease or bone disorders.

Amenorrhea
Absence of a menstrual cycle for women within the reproductive age.

American Psychiatric Association (APA)
Professional organization of psychiatrists

American Psychological Association (APA)
A scientific and professional organization that represents psychologists in the United States.

Anemia
A condition that develops when blood lacks enough healthy red blood cells or hemoglobin. Hemoglobin is a main part of red blood cells and binds oxygen. When there are too few or abnormal red blood cells, or hemoglobin is abnormal or low, the cells in one's body will not get enough oxygen.

Anna Westin Act
Law passed in 2015 that provided more funding for health-care professionals and school personnel with the intention of enabling earlier intervention strategies and action for eating disorders.

Anorexia mirabilis
A term that refers to loss of appetite and has biological parallels to anorexia. This term became well known in medical texts in the 19th century, when a disease classification system was created.

Anorexia nervosa
An eating disorder characterized by weight loss (or lack of appropriate weight gain in growing children); difficulties maintaining an appropriate body weight for height, age, and stature; and, in many individuals, distorted body image.

Aspartate transaminase
AST is an enzyme found in cells throughout the body but mostly in the heart and liver and, to a lesser extent, in the kidneys and muscles. In healthy individuals, levels of AST in the blood are low. When liver or muscle cells are injured, they release AST into the blood.

Avoidant/restrictive food intake disorder
ARFID was introduced as a new diagnostic category in the *DSM*-5. The ARFID diagnosis describes individuals whose symptoms do not match the criteria for traditional ED diagnoses, but who, nonetheless, experience clinically significant struggles with eating and food. Symptoms of ARFID typically show up in infancy or childhood, but they may also present or persist into adulthood.

Bilirubin
A yellow compound that occurs in the normal catabolic pathway that breaks down heme in vertebrates. This catabolism is a necessary process in the body's clearance of waste products that arise from the destruction of aged or abnormal red blood cells.

Binge eating disorder
BED is a severe, life-threatening, and treatable eating disorder characterized by recurrent episodes of eating large quantities of food (often very quickly and to the point of discomfort); a feeling of a loss of control during the binge; experiencing shame, distress or guilt afterward; and not regularly using unhealthy compensatory measures (e.g., purging) to counter the binge eating. It is the most common eating disorder in the United States.

Body mass index
BMI is one's weight-to-height ratio.

Bruch, Hilde
A German-born American doctor and psychoanalyst whose most popular publication, *The Golden Cage: The Enigma of Anorexia Nervosa,* prompted a significant shift in awareness around the prevalence of anorexia.

Bulimia nervosa
A serious, potentially life-threatening eating disorder characterized by a cycle of bingeing and compensatory behaviors such as self-induced vomiting designed to undo or compensate for the effects of binge eating.

Carpenter, Karen
Lead singer of the Carpenters. Karen's struggle with an eating disorder was one of the first viewed in the public eye. She died in 1983 at the age of 32 due to cardiac complications related to her eating disorder.

Catherine of Siena
A well-known saint who engaged in fasting for religious reasons during one of the first starvation outbreaks. Her story influenced multiple female followers, some of whom passed away from fasting behaviors.

Chlorosis
Also known as the "green sickness" by the English, this condition was said to have occurred during a female's transition from puberty to sexual maturity. Symptoms included loss of appetite, amenorrhea, and mood changes.

Chronicity
Unrelenting and long-lasting cycle of symptoms.

Cognitive behavioral therapy
CBT, a relatively short-term, symptom-oriented therapy focusing on the beliefs, values, and cognitive processes that maintain the ED behavior. CBT aims to modify distorted beliefs and attitudes.

Comorbidity
When two disorders occur at the same time.

Compensatory behaviors
Behaviors intended to make up for the intake of calories, such as vomiting, misuse of laxatives, and so forth.

Corset
An article of clothing designed to help shape a woman's body into a thinner figure. Despite the physical discomfort and pain, many women wore them daily.

Creatinine
A waste product from the normal breakdown of muscle tissue. As creatinine is produced, it's filtered through the kidneys and excreted in urine. Doctors measure the blood creatinine level as a test of kidney function.

Destigmatization
Removing associations of shame or disgrace from.

Diabulimia
A media-coined term that refers to an eating disorder in a person with diabetes, typically type 1 diabetes, wherein the person purposefully restricts insulin in order to lose weight. Some medical professionals use the term ED-DMT1, eating disorder-diabetes mellitus type 1, which is used to refer to any type of eating disorder comorbid with type 1 diabetes.

Diagnostic and Statistical Manual of Mental Disorders (*DSM*)
A classification system of all mental disorders that serves as a platform for mental health clinicians to diagnose and treat mental health disorders.

Dialectical behavior therapy
DBT is a type of psychotherapy originally developed by Marsha Linehan specific to treating borderline personality disorder. This treatment modality is now utilized for a variety of disorders and aims to help an individual implement skills centered around four main areas: mindfulness, distress tolerance, emotion regulation, and interpersonal effectiveness.

Differential diagnosis
The process of differentiating between two or more conditions that share similar signs or symptoms.

Disordered eating
Refers to eating patterns or behaviors that resemble symptoms of an eating disorder; however, altogether, the frequency, intensity, and severity are not enough to warrant the diagnosis of an eating disorder.

DNA methylation
A process that alters the activity of DNA rather than the DNA sequence.

DSM task force
A group of experts in clinical practice and research who were brought together to direct and make recommended changes for the *DSM*-5.

Eating disorder not otherwise specified
EDNOS is the term used in a previous *DSM* to describe an eating disorder that did not fall into the category of anorexia or bulimia.

Eating Disorders Coalition
The EDC is an avenue for building awareness among politicians and proposing new congressional bills aimed to advocate and provide greater access to treatment for those with an eating disorder.

Electrocardiogram
An ECG or EKG is a test that checks how the heart is functioning by measuring its electrical activity. With each heartbeat, an electrical impulse (or wave) travels through the heart. This wave causes the muscle to squeeze and pump blood.

Electrolytes
Minerals in the body that have an electric charge. They are in blood, urine, tissues, and other body fluids. Electrolytes are important because they help balance the amount of water in the body and balance its acid/base (pH) level.

Epigenetics
An area of study that looks at certain biological processes that can turn a gene off and on.

Estrogen
Primary female sex hormone.

Fad diet
Recommended meal plans or trends that promote results most often aimed at weight loss or health advantages but are often dangerous to one's health. Examples include the ketogenic, low-carb, and paleo diets.

Fasting
Self-denial of all food and/or drink for a specified period of time. In some cases, the amount of food or liquid is simply reduced.

Gastrointestinal
Relating to the stomach and the intestines.

Gull, Sir William Withey
A pioneer in defining anorexia as a full-scale illness and bringing it closer within the fields of science and medicine

Harm avoidance
A personality trait characterized by excessive worrying; pessimism; shyness; and being fearful, doubtful, and easily fatigued.

Harm-reduction approach
Framework for treating chronic addictions and disorders, including eating disorders, that aims to minimize symptoms as much as possible in order to treat the consequences for a long period of time.

Health at Every Size® (HAES) approach
An approach that aims to illuminate the idea that health includes more than just physical attributes.

Heritability
Amount of variation in a trait that can be credited to genetic factors.

Hypoglycemia
Low blood glucose levels.

Hypokalemia
Low potassium levels.

Hypotonia
Low muscle tone (the amount of tension or resistance to stretch in a muscle), often involving reduced muscle strength.

International Classification of Diseases (ICD)
Maps health conditions and assigns a specific diagnostic code. The *ICD* is maintained by the World Health Organization.

Lapse
A more pronounced and longer slip with regard to ED behaviors. The individual is able to interrupt this lapse in order to get back on track.

Lasègue, Ernest-Charles
A pioneer in defining anorexia as a full-scale illness and bringing it closer within the fields of science and medicine.

Latinx
Latinx is a gender-neutral term sometimes used in lieu of Latino or Latina (referencing cultural or racial identity).

LIVE Well Act
A health-centered act focused on ED prevention. This act focuses on health instead of just weight, and it aims to identify those at risk for developing disordered eating behaviors and/or an eating disorder.

Molecular genetics
Examination of the structure and function of genes on a molecular level.

Morton, Richard
Writer of a narrative on "nervous consumption" in 1689 and one of the first to put a name to the condition we now define as anorexia nervosa.

Night eating syndrome
An eating disorder characterized by a delayed circadian pattern of food intake.

Orthorexia nervosa
Although not formally recognized in the *Diagnostic and Statistical Manual*, the term was coined in 1998 and means an obsession with proper or healthful eating.

Osteopenia
Signifies low bone density and strength but is reversible. Prolonged symptoms can lead to osteoporosis.

Osteoporosis
Permanent bone weakness that increases one's chance for fractures and breaks

Other specified feeding and eating disorders
Previously known as Eating disorder not otherwise specified (EDNOS) in past editions of the *Diagnostic and Statistical Manual*. The category was developed to encompass those individuals who did not meet strict diagnostic criteria for anorexia nervosa or bulimia nervosa but still had a significant eating disorder. In community clinics, the majority of individuals were historically diagnosed with EDNOS.

Pharmacological
Relating to the branch of medicine involving drugs.

Pica
An eating disorder that involves eating items that are not typically thought of as food and that do not contain significant nutritional value, such as hair, dirt, and paint chips.

Presentation
Display of symptoms.

Psychopathology
A mental or behavioral disorder.

Purge
In relation to eating disorders, purging can include self-induced vomiting, laxative or diuretic abuse, enemas, and compulsive exercise in an attempt to cleanse, purify, rid, clear, or free the body of food.

Refeeding syndrome
Condition that occurs when the intake of food causes a change in fluids and electrolytes. As a result, the body has to work harder than it is capable of doing at that time, which can then dangerously impact potassium and phosphorus levels.

Relapse
A person meets full criteria for a type of eating disorder again.

Restriction
Decreasing or eliminating specific food items or amounts of food from one's daily intake. This is a subtype of anorexia nervosa and one of the main criteria for the diagnosis.

Serotonin
A chemical and neurotransmitter in the human body that impacts sleep, mood, digestion, and other functions.

Sleep apnea
A serious sleep condition during which breathing patterns become irregular.

Slip
A deviation from one's recovery-focused routine, meal plan, exercise regimen, and the like. The individual is able to rebound from this urge or behavioral change without significant alterations in the recovery process.

Stunkard, Albert
Renowned psychiatrist who first spoke of binge eating symptoms in 1959.

Taylor, Martha
A 19-year-old girl whose story of starvation and survival was one of the first documented.

Temperament
A person's nature, especially as it permanently affects the person's behavior.

Trait
A genetically determined characteristic.

21st Century Cures Act
Act passed by Congress in 2016 and aims to provide more training for professionals in order to identify and treat symptoms earlier.

Type 2 diabetes
A condition that occurs when the body becomes resistant to insulin.

Urinalysis
A test done on urine to detect and manage a wide range of disorders, such as urinary tract infections, kidney disease, and diabetes. A urinalysis involves checking the appearance, concentration, and content of urine.

Westernization
The assimilation of Western culture; the social process of becoming familiar with or converting to the customs and practices of Western civilization.

World Health Organization
WHO is the specialized agency of the United Nations system that is centered upon international public health.

Directory of Resources

BOOKS ON EATING DISORDERS

Armstrong, Stephanie Covington. *Not All Black Girls Know How to Eat.* Chicago: Lawrence Hill Books, 2009.

Brown, Harriet. *Brave Girl Eating: A Family's Struggle with Anorexia.* New York: William Morrow, 2010.

Brown, Harriet, ed. *Feed Me! Writers Dish about Food, Eating, Weight, and Body Image.* New York: Ballantine Books, 2009.

Brumberg, Joan Jacobs. *The Body Project.* New York: Vintage Books, 1997.

Brumberg, Joan Jacobs. *Fasting Girls: The History of Anorexia Nervosa.* New York: Vintage Books, 1988.

Cohen, Mary Anne. *French Toast for Breakfast: Declaring Peace with Emotional Eating.* Carlsbad, CA: Gürze Books, 1995.

Costin, Carolyn. *The Eating Disorder Sourcebook.* New York: McGraw-Hill Education, 2006.

De Rossi, Portia. *Unbearable Lightness: A Story of Loss and Gain.* New York: Atria Books, 2010.

Edut, Ophira, ed. *Body Outlaws: Rewriting the Rules of Beauty and Body Image.* Emeryville, CA: Seal Press, 2004.

Frank, Guido K. W. *What Causes Eating Disorders—And What Do They Cause?* St. Petersburg, FL: Booklocker.com, Inc., 2016.

Gaudini, Jennifer L. *Sick Enough.* New York: Routledge, 2018.

Gay, Roxanne. *Hunger: A Memoir of (My) Body.* New York: Harper Collins Publishers, 2017.

Holme, Natasha. *Lesbian Crushes and Bulimia: A Diary on How I Acquired My Eating Disorder.* Scotts Valley, CA: CreateSpace Independent Publishing, 2014.

Hornbacher, Marya. *Wasted: A Memoir of Anorexia and Bulimia.* New York: HarpPeren, 2006.

Johnson, Anita. *Eating in the Light of the Moon.* Carlsbad, CA: Gürze Books, 1996.

Liu, Aimee. *Gaining: The Truth about Life after Eating Disorders.* New York: Warner Books, 2007.

Mitchell, Andie. *It Was Me All Along.* New York: Clarkson Potter Publishers, 2015.

Phillips, Katharine A. *The Broken Mirror.* Oxford: Oxford University Press, 1996.

Schaefer, Jenni. *Goodbye ED, Hello Me.* New York: McGraw-Hill Education, 2009.

Schaefer, Jenni. *Life without ED.* New York: McGraw-Hill Education, 2004.

Schauster, Heidi. *Nourish: How to Heal Your Relationship with Food.* Brush, CO: Hummingbird Press, 2018.

Thompson, Becky W. *A Hunger So Wide and So Deep: A Multi-Racial View of Women's Eating Problems.* Minneapolis: University of Minnesota Press, 1994.

Van Der Kolk, Bessel. *The Body Keeps the Score.* New York: Penguin Books, 2014.

SUPPORT AND RESEARCH ORGANIZATIONS

Academy of Eating Disorders (AED)

AED is a global professional association committed to leadership in eating disorders research, education, treatment, and prevention.

Website: https://www.aedweb.org/home

American Psychological Association (APA)

APA is a scientific and professional organization that represents psychologists in the United States.

Website: http://www.apa.org

Binge Eating Disorder Association (BEDA)

BEDA is a national organization centered upon providing support and advocacy for those struggling with binge eating disorder. It focuses on education regarding diagnosis and treatment with the intention to increase awareness and enhance levels of support for this type of eating disorder.

Eating Disorder Foundation (EDF)

The mission of EDF is to be an effective resource in the prevention and elimination of eating disorders through education, support, and advocacy.

Website: https://www.eatingdisorderfoundation.org

Eating Disorder Hope (EDH)

EDH offers education, support, and inspiration to ED sufferers, their loved ones, and eating disorders treatment providers.

Website: https://www.eatingdisorderhope.com

Eating Disorders Anonymous (EDA)

EDA is a fellowship of individuals who share their experience, strength, and hope with each other in order that they may solve their common problems and help others to recover from their eating disorders.

Website: http://www.eatingdisordersanonymous.org

Eating Disorders Coalition (EDC)

EDC advances the recognition of eating disorders as a public health priority by building relationships with Congress, federal agencies, and countless national and local organizations dedicated to health issues.

Website: https://www.eatingdisorderscoalition.org

Foundation for Research and Education in Eating Disorders (FREED)

The mission of FREED is to help determine the causes and risk factors associated with developing eating disorders, facilitate the development of treatments, and promote education, prevention, and recovery from these illnesses.

Website: https://www.freedeatingdisorders.org

International Association of Eating Disorders Professionals (iaedp)

The iaedp is recognized for its excellence in providing first-quality education and high-level training standards to an international, multidisciplinary group of various health-care treatment providers and helping professions who treat the full spectrum of ED problems.

Website: http://www.iaedp.com

Multi-Service Eating Disorder Association (MEDA)

MEDA provides education about eating disorders as well as a network of treatment providers and resources intended to develop a compassionate community that promotes hopefulness and supports healing.

Website: https://www.medainc.org

National Alliance on Mental Illness (NAMI)

NAMI is the nation's largest grassroots mental health organization dedicated to building better lives for the millions of Americans affected by mental illness.

Website: https://www.nami.org

National Association of Anorexia Nervosa and Associated Disorders (ANAD)

ANAD is a nonprofit (501c3) organization working in the areas of support, awareness, advocacy, referral, education, and prevention.

Website: http://anad.org

National Eating Disorders Association (NEDA)

NEDA supports individuals and families affected by eating disorders, and it serves as a catalyst for prevention, cures, and access to quality care.

Website: https://www.nationaleatingdisorders.org

National Institute of Mental Health (NIMH)

NIMH is a part of the US Department of Health and Human Services and is the lead federal agency for research on mental disorders. It is one of the 27 institutes and centers that make up the National Institutes of Health (NIH), the largest biomedical research agency in the world.

Website: https://www.nimh.nih.gov/index.shtml

Overeaters Anonymous (OA)

OA is a fellowship of individuals who, through shared experience, strength, and hope, are recovering from compulsive overeating.

Website: https://oa.org

World Health Organization (WHO)

WHO works worldwide to promote health, keep the world safe, and serve the vulnerable with a goal to ensure that a billion more people have universal health coverage, to protect a billion more people from health emergencies, and provide a further billion people with better health and well-being.

Website: https://www.who.int

WEBSITES/BLOGS

Mirror Mirror

This website was originally created by a woman who was recovering from an eating disorder and was hoping to provide education and support for others with eating disorders while also educating herself and working through some of the issues that she struggled with personally.

Website: https://www.mirror-mirror.org

Project HEAL

Project HEAL is an organization described as "America's strongest voice that full recovery from an eating disorder is possible and should be accessible." With chapters worldwide, they aim to acquire knowledge and research about ED recovery from both personal and professional sources in order to access complete recovery.

Website: https://www.theprojectheal.org

Something Fishy

The website is dedicated to raising awareness about eating disorders, emphasizing always that eating disorders are *not* about food and weight but are the symptoms of something deeper going on inside. Something Fishy is determined to remind all individuals impacted by anorexia, bulimia, compulsive overeating, and binge eating disorder that they are not alone and that complete recovery is possible.

Website: http://www.something-fishy.org

Southern Smash

The website is devoted to "raising eating disorder awareness & spreading body love one SMASH at a time." Southern Smash aims to shift a disturbing "new normal" and begin a different conversation around our bodies, self-love, and self-worth as well as provide knowledge about the detriments of an eating disorder.

Website: https://www.southernsmash.org

Index

About the Authors

Dr. Jessica Bartley is a clinical assistant professor in the sport and performance psychology program and the director of the Center for Performance Excellence at the University of Denver. She is also contracted as a sport psychologist with several Olympic athletes and teams through the United States Olympic Committee and is a member of a group private practice focused on sport and performance consulting. Dr. Bartley holds an MA in sport and performance psychology (2008) as well as a doctorate in clinical psychology (2012) with an emphasis in sport and performance psychology and behavioral therapy from the University of Denver.

Dr. Melissa Streno is a clinical psychologist at EDCare, an ED treatment facility in Denver, Colorado. She is also an adjunct professor in sport and performance psychology in the Graduate School of Professional Psychology at the University of Denver and is part of a group private practice focused on sport and performance consulting. Dr. Streno earned her PsyD in clinical psychology in 2015 from the University of Denver's Graduate School of Professional Psychology. She also earned an MA in sport and performance psychology (2010) from the University of Denver.

www.ingramcontent.com/pod-product-compliance
Lightning Source LLC
Chambersburg PA
CBHW050526270326
41926CB00015B/3086